Comptroller's Handbook

A-CRE

I0448279

Safety and Soundness

| Capital Adequacy (C) | Asset Quality (A) | Management (M) | Earnings (E) | Liquidity (L) | Sensitivity to Market Risk (S) | Other Activities (O) |

Commercial Real Estate Lending

August 2013

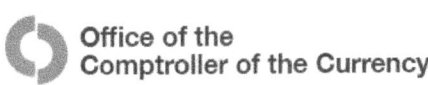

Office of the Comptroller of the Currency

Washington, DC 20219

Contents

Introduction

The Office of the Comptroller of the Currency's (OCC) *Comptroller's Handbook* booklet, "Commercial Real Estate Lending," provides guidance for bank examiners and bankers on commercial real estate (CRE) lending activities. For the purposes of this booklet, CRE lending comprises acquisition, development, and construction (ADC) financing and the financing of income-producing real estate. Income-producing real estate comprises real estate held for lease to third parties and nonresidential real estate that is occupied by its owner or a related party.

The booklet addresses the risks inherent in CRE lending as well as risks unique to specific lending activities and property types. Also discussed are supervisory expectations and regulatory requirements for prudent risk management.

The booklet includes expanded examination procedures to assist examiners in completing bank core assessments that are affected by CRE lending. The procedures include an internal control questionnaire and verification procedures to further support the examination process.

Throughout this booklet, national banks and federal savings associations are referred to collectively as banks, except when it is necessary to distinguish between the two.

Overview

Background

CRE lending is an important line of business for the banking industry, and CRE activities contribute significantly to the U.S. economy. Many banks rely on revenue from this business to grow and prosper. History has shown, however, that imprudent risk taking and inadequate risk management, particularly during periods of rapid economic growth, can lead to significant losses and be a major cause of bank failures.

One of the key elements of risk in this type of lending is the cyclical nature of real estate markets where, as markets peak and decline, banks with large concentrations of CRE loans may suffer considerable distress. While the banking industry cannot accurately predict or control the timing of the real estate business cycle, banks that demonstrate faithful adherence to prudent lending practices and regulatory guidance can keep losses from CRE lending to a manageable level, even when markets experience significant stress.

Authority and Limits

Banks are permitted by statute to engage in real estate lending. The authority for national banks is found in 12 USC 371, while the authority for federal savings associations is found in 12 USC 1464. Both national banks and federal savings associations are subject to a uniform rule on real estate lending, which incorporates the "Interagency Guidelines for Real Estate

Lending Policies." This rule can be found in 12 CFR 34, subpart D for national banks and in 12 CFR 160.101 for federal savings associations.

No aggregate exposure limit applies to a national bank's real estate lending activities, as long as the volume and nature of the lending does not pose unwarranted risk to the bank's financial condition. Permissible real estate exposures for federal savings associations are described in 12 USC 1464 of the Home Owner's Loan Act (HOLA). 12 USC 1464(c)(1)(B) authorizes federal savings associations to invest in residential real estate loans, including multifamily residential real estate loans, without limit provided the volume and nature of the lending does not pose unwarranted risk to the federal savings association's financial condition. Nonresidential real estate lending is limited under 12 USC 1464(c)(2)(B) to 400 percent of total capital[1] (note, however, that concentration concerns may arise with aggregate exposure of substantially less than 400 percent of capital).[2] A federal savings association that makes a loan secured by nonresidential real estate also has the option to classify that loan as a commercial loan as authorized under 12 USC 1464(c)(2)(A).[3]

Real Estate Markets

Real estate is a highly cyclical industry that is affected by changes in local and national economic conditions. Although national conditions affect the overall real estate industry, how national conditions influence local conditions is most important. Factors such as rates of employment, consumer demand, household formation, and the level of economic activity can vary widely from state to state and among metropolitan areas, cities, and towns. Metropolitan markets comprise various submarkets where property values and demand can be affected by many factors, such as demographic makeup, geographic features, transportation, recreation, local government, school systems, utility infrastructure, tax burden, building-stock age, zoning and building codes, and available land for development.

In addition to geographic considerations, markets can be defined by property type. A bank's CRE lending strategy may target one or more of the five primary real estate sectors:

---

[1] Without regard to any limitations of this part, a federal savings association may make or invest in the fully insured or guaranteed portion of nonresidential real estate loans insured or guaranteed by the Economic Development Administration, the Farmers Home Administration or its successor the Farm Service Agency, or the Small Business Administration. Unguaranteed portions of guaranteed loans must be aggregated with uninsured loans when determining an association's compliance with the 400 percent of capital limitation for other real estate loans.

[2] The OCC may approve an exception to the nonresidential real estate lending limit pursuant to 1464(c)(2)(B)(ii) upon the OCC's determination that the exception poses no significant risk to safe and sound operation and is consistent with prudent operating practice. If an exception is granted, the OCC will closely monitor the federal savings association's condition and lending activities to ensure that nonresidential real estate loans are made in a safe and sound manner in compliance with all relevant laws and regulations.

[3] Under 12 CFR 1464(c)(2)(A), federal savings associations may invest up to 20 percent of their assets in commercial loans, provided that amounts in excess of 10 percent of total assets may be used only for small business loans.

office, retail, industrial, hospitality, and residential, which includes multifamily and one- to four-family development and construction. While all sectors are influenced by economic conditions, some sectors are more sensitive to certain economic factors than others. The demand for office space depends on office-related employment, which tends to be concentrated in the finance, insurance, technology, and real estate industries, as well as some categories of services, particularly business services. The demand for retail space is affected by local employment levels and consumer spending. Demand for industrial space tends to be influenced by proximity to labor, transportation infrastructure, local tax rates, and the presence of a similar or related industry. The hospitality sector is affected locally by the level of business activity but is also influenced by consumer spending, the cost of travel and the strength of the U.S. dollar. In the residential sector, demand is heavily influenced by the local quality of life, demographics, affordability of homeownership, the rate of household formations, and local employment conditions.

Banks are expected to monitor the conditions in the markets where they are active and consider them in their monitoring and lending strategies.

Risks Associated With CRE Lending

From a supervisory perspective, risk is the potential that events, expected or unexpected, will have an adverse effect on a bank's earnings, capital, or franchise or enterprise value. The OCC has defined eight categories of risk for bank supervision purposes: credit, interest rate, liquidity, price, operational, compliance, strategic, and reputation. These categories are not mutually exclusive. Any product or service may expose a bank to multiple risks. Risks also may be interdependent and may be positively or negatively correlated. Examiners should be aware of this interdependence and assess the effect in a consistent and inclusive manner. Refer to the "Bank Supervision Process" booklet of the *Comptroller's Handbook* for an expanded discussion of banking risks and their definitions.

The risks associated with CRE lending in particular are credit, interest rate, liquidity, operational, compliance, strategic, and reputation. The OCC expects banks to appropriately identify, measure, monitor, and control risk by implementing an effective risk management system. When examiners assess the effectiveness of a bank's risk management system, they consider its policies, processes, personnel, and control systems.

Credit Risk

Factors that can affect a bank's likelihood of receiving repayment as expected for loans financing CRE include the following.

Construction issues: Banks that finance construction assume the risk associated with a borrower's ability to successfully complete a proposed project on time and within budget. Budget overruns can result in total costs that exceed the property's value when completed. Overruns may be caused by inaccurate budgets, increases in materials or transportation expenses, material or labor shortages, substandard work performed by the borrower's employees or subcontractors that must be redone to satisfy contract performance conditions or to meet local building codes, increased interest expense, or delays caused by inclement weather. Projects that rehabilitate or extensively modify existing buildings can be exceptionally vulnerable to overruns because costs in these cases are more difficult to project.

Market conditions: A property's performance can be negatively affected by tenants' deteriorating credit strength and lease expirations in times of softening demand caused by economic deterioration or over-supply conditions. As the economic climate deteriorates, tenants may reduce their space or cease operations and the payment of rent altogether. Properties that have shorter lease terms are vulnerable to declining market values as rents decline and leases are renewed at lower rental rates. Leases with longer lease terms may also become vulnerable in softening markets as tenants seek to negotiate the renewal of their leases early to take advantage of the lower rates. As expiring leases cause project cash flows to decline, developers may be unable to meet scheduled mortgage payments and other important obligations, such as property taxes and maintenance. Even if borrowers are able to meet their payment obligations, they may find it difficult to refinance their full loan amounts at maturity due to declines in property value.

The risk from changing market conditions can be considerable in ADC financing of for-sale developments. Adverse changes in the market occurring between the start of development and completion can result in slower sales rates and lower sales prices that could threaten timely and full repayment. Risk posed by changing market conditions is magnified to the extent that portfolio concentrations of CRE are present.

Regulatory changes: At the national or local level, changes in tax legislation, zoning, environmental regulation, or similar external conditions may affect property values and the economic feasibility of existing and proposed real estate projects.

Interest rates: Interest rates affect the cost of construction and the financial viability of a real estate project. When a project has floating rate debt and fixed rents, increasing interest rates may have a negative effect on repayment capacity. Higher interest rates may also result in higher capitalization rates, thereby reducing a property's value. While borrowers can hedge their interest rate risk sensitivity by using interest rate derivatives, mitigation is difficult for construction facilities due to the changes in the outstanding loan amount during development.

Environmental liability: Contamination may decrease the collateral's value or render the collateral worthless. Furthermore, the cost that may be imposed on a responsible borrower for the remediation of a contaminated property may severely impair the borrower's ability to repay the loan.

Interest Rate Risk

The level of interest rate risk attributed to the bank's CRE lending activities depends on the composition of its loan portfolio and the degree to which the structure of its loans, such as tenor, pricing, and amortization, expose the bank's revenue to changes in interest rates.

Much of the CRE financing provided by banks is on a floating-rate basis, meaning the interest rate sensitivity for the lending bank, is relatively low. Banks that provide fixed-rate financing for extended terms, however, expose themselves to interest rate risk to the extent that these loans are funded by shorter-term liabilities.

Liquidity Risk

CRE loans are ordinarily illiquid. The conversion of CRE loans to cash can be accomplished by (1) refinancing the loan with another lender; (2) through the sale of the loan to an investor (either on a participation, whole-loan, or portfolio basis);[4] (3) by securitizing the loan; (4) through normal repayment by the borrower; or (5) by serving as collateral for borrowings.[5]

Sales of CRE loans are difficult to execute largely because of their lack of homogeneity. Unlike consumer loans, the due diligence process can be time-consuming and expensive for a prospective purchaser because of variations in property type, location desirability, tenant quality and other rent roll characteristics, underwriting, loan structures and, documentation. CRE loans tend to be even less liquid in times of market stress, when potential funding sources diminish as lenders allocate fewer funds for real estate. This can make the sale of loans or their refinance by other lenders as a strategy to manage concentrations ineffective. ADC loans are particularly illiquid because of their short tenor and because the full collateral value is not realized until the project is completed and reaches a stabilized level of occupancy or is ready for sale.

While securitization can provide liquidity, CRE loans originated for securitization employ underwriting, structures, and documentation that conform to standards established by market participants. This standardization permits a more efficient due diligence process and results in better pricing. Loans originated to be held in the bank's portfolio typically do not meet the standards for this market, making securitization of these assets inefficient and likely to result in prices that represent a material discount to book value. Market disruptions after origination and before sale can reduce the liquidity of loans that were originated for securitization.

Operational Risk

While operational risk exists in all products and services, CRE lending, particularly for ADC, presents higher operational risk than many other types of lending. Banks need effective systems for monitoring property performance and the progress of construction and for controlling the disbursement of loan proceeds and repayment. Banks must have systems in place to protect their interests in collateral by ensuring that property taxes, property insurance premiums, and workers and suppliers are paid. Ineffective systems can introduce significant

---

[4] The "Loan Portfolio Management" booklet of the *Comptroller's Handbook* provides guidance on loan participations.

[5] Qualifying CRE loans may collateralize borrowings from the Federal Reserve or Federal Home Loan Banks. See the "Liquidity" booklet of the *Comptroller's Handbook* for a discussion of asset liquidity including secured borrowings.

operational risks. Strategies for controlling the operational risks associated with these activities are discussed later in this "Introduction" section.

Compliance Risk

Banks' CRE lending is governed by the statutes and regulations described in this booklet. Failure to comply with them can present serious risk to earnings and capital. Unlike consumer transactions, there are few borrower-focused regulations that address CRE financing. Real estate as collateral is subject, however, to compliance with building codes, zoning requirements, flood insurance, and other government regulations.

While environmental contamination can threaten loan repayment, as discussed in the "Credit Risk" section of this booklet, failure to ensure compliance with environmental laws and regulations can generate significant liability to a bank that is over and above the value of the collateral. While this liability typically manifests itself when a bank takes title to the collateral in satisfaction of debt, a bank most often sows the seeds of this risk at origination by failure to comply with the laws and regulations governing contaminated properties that are discussed later in this booklet.

Strategic Risk

A sound CRE lending program requires management and staff who have the knowledge and experience to identify, measure, monitor, and control the risks unique to real estate. Failure to provide effective oversight of CRE lending activities can increase a bank's strategic risk profile while also affecting interdependent risks, such as credit and reputation risks.

Reputation Risk

Failure to meet the needs of the community, inefficient loan delivery systems, and lender liability lawsuits are some of the factors that may tarnish the bank's reputation. Imprudent risk taking in CRE lending can cause a bank to experience excessive losses or to foreclose on assets, rendering the bank unable to continue providing needed real estate financing in the market it serves.

Risk Management

Real Estate Lending Standards

National banks and federal savings associations are subject to a uniform rule on real estate lending that is documented in subpart D of 12 CFR 34 (national banks) and 12 CFR 160.101 (federal savings associations). The rule requires banks to adopt written real estate lending policies that are consistent with safe and sound banking practices. The rule applies to all extensions of credit that are secured by liens on or interests in real estate. It also includes loans made for the purpose of financing the construction of a building or other improvements whether or not secured by real estate. The real estate lending policies should be appropriate for the bank's size and the nature and scope of its operations and should reflect the level of risk that is acceptable to its board of directors. The board of directors must review and approve the bank's real estate lending policy at least annually.

Specifically, the regulations require banks to

- establish loan portfolio diversification standards.
- establish prudent underwriting standards, including loan-to-value (LTV) limits that are clear and measurable.
- establish loan administration procedures for the real estate portfolio.
- establish documentation, approval, and reporting requirements to monitor compliance with the bank's real estate lending policy.
- monitor conditions in the bank's real estate lending market to ensure that its lending policies continue to be appropriate for current market conditions.

In addition, the regulations specify that a bank's real estate lending policy should reflect consideration of the "Interagency Guidelines for Real Estate Lending Policies," which are contained in appendix A of subpart D of 12 CFR 34 (national banks) and in the appendix to 12 CFR 160.101 (federal savings associations). These guidelines describe key elements of a real estate lending policy including

- loan portfolio management considerations.
- underwriting standards.
- loan administration.
- LTV limits.
- exceptions to general lending policy.

The following sections provide an overview of each of the five elements presented above.

Loan Portfolio Management Considerations

Consistent with a bank's strategic plan, a bank's real estate lending policy should describe the scope and nature of its lending activities. The policy should include how real estate loans are extended and serviced. When formulating its loan policy, a bank should consider the

- size and financial condition of the bank.
- lending staff's expertise and loan administration capabilities.
- process for managing concentrations.
- requirement to comply with applicable laws and regulations.
- market conditions and supply and demand trends in real estate markets.

In addition, the real estate lending policy should

- identify the geographic markets in which the bank considers lending.
- establish a portfolio diversification strategy and set limits for real estate loans by type, purpose, LTV, borrower, tenor, etc.
- develop appropriate terms and conditions for each type of loan.
- maintain procedures for loan approval, origination, disbursements, and collections.
- establish prudent, clear, and measurable underwriting standards, including LTV limits that reflect consideration of supervisory LTV (SLTV) guidelines.
- adopt review, approval, and reporting procedures for loans that are exceptions to policy, including loans that exceed SLTV limits.
- establish loan administration procedures for maintaining legal and account maintenance documentation, disbursements, collateral inspections, collection, and loan review.
- adopt an effective appraisal and evaluation program that reflects compliance with 12 CFR 34, subpart C (national banks) or 12 CFR 164 (federal savings associations), and related guidance.
- develop management information reporting procedures for the board of directors or designated committees thereof and management.

Banks' policies and practices should reflect consideration of risks posed by individual loans as well as aggregate portfolio risk. Even when individual loans are prudently underwritten, groups of loans that are similarly affected by internal and external market factors may expose banks to a heightened level of risk that may warrant management attention and additional capital support.

Underwriting Standards

Underwriting standards that are clear and measurable should be stated in the policy to guide the lending staff when evaluating credit risk associated with transactions. Prudently underwritten real estate loans should reflect relevant credit considerations, including the following.

Debt-service coverage: Cash flow from the underlying property or other indicators of borrower capacity should be evaluated to determine to what extent the borrower can adequately service interest and principal on a prospective loan. Banks should establish minimum debt-service coverage ratio (DSCR) guidelines that would be considered acceptable for each type of loan transaction.

LTV: The market value of existing properties and properties to be developed should be established in accordance with 12 CFR 34, subpart C (national banks) or 12 CFR 164 (federal savings associations), and related guidelines. Banks should establish appropriate LTV guidelines for each type of loan transaction that reflect consideration of the SLTV guidelines discussed in the "LTV Limits" section of this booklet. In addition to the value of the existing or proposed real estate, banks should consider the value provided by any readily marketable collateral or other acceptable collateral in determining LTV criteria.

Creditworthiness: Banks should maintain standards for evaluating the creditworthiness of borrowers and the support provided by guarantees, if applicable. Evaluations should include analysis of the borrower's or guarantor's global financial condition including assets (type, amount, and liquidity), global cash flow, and direct and contingent liabilities, as well as any tertiary repayment sources that may be available to a bank in the event of recourse.

Borrower equity: Banks should establish hard equity (e.g., cash or unencumbered investment in the underlying property) guidelines for various types of lending transactions. An analysis of borrower equity should be clearly documented as part of the credit file.

Credit enhancements: The underwriting process should include an analysis of credit enhancements such as mortgage insurance, take-out commitments, or repayment guarantees from external sources.

For each loan program or property type, the bank's policy should specify

- maximum loan commitment amount.
- minimum debt-service coverage expectations.
- maximum LTV.
- maximum loan tenor.
- amortization criteria.
- pricing and profitability objectives.

In addition, for both ADC loans and loans financing existing commercial properties, bank policy should establish expectations for evaluating

- project feasibility and sensitivity to changes in economic conditions, including the sensitivity of projections to changes in market variables, such as interest rates, vacancy rates, and operating expenses.
- environmental risk.
- minimum requirements for initial investment and maintenance of hard equity by the borrower.
- minimum standards for net worth, cash flow, and debt-service coverage of the borrower or the project.
- standards for the acceptability of and limits on nonamortizing loans.
- standards for the acceptability of and limits on the use of interest reserves.
- preleasing requirements for income-producing property.
- presale and minimum release requirements for tract development financing.
- limits on partial and nonrecourse loans.

- requirements for takeout commitments.
- loan covenant requirements.

Loan Administration

Banks should establish real estate loan administration procedures, including

- documentation standards such as requirements for receipt, frequency, verification and maintenance of financial statements and other information provided by the borrower.
- types and frequency of collateral valuations.
- loan closing and disbursements controls.
- payment processing.
- escrow administration.
- collateral administration.
- loan payoffs.
- delinquency and collections.
- deed-in-lieu of foreclosure.
- claims processing.
- seeking satisfaction from a financial guarantor or insurance.
- servicing and loan participation guidelines.

LTV Limits

Each bank should establish its own internal LTV limits which should not exceed the SLTV guidelines shown in the following table.

SLTV Limits by Loan Category

Loan category	SLTV limit (less than or equal to)
Raw land	65%
Land development or improved lots	75%
Construction	
Commercial, multifamily,[a] and other nonresidential	80%
One- to four-family residential	85%
Improved property—commercial, multifamily, and other nonresidential	85%
Owner-occupied one- to four-family and home equity	90%[b]

[a] Multifamily construction includes condominiums and cooperatives.

[b] An LTV limit has not been established for permanent mortgage or home equity loans on owner-occupied, one- to four-family residential property; however, for any such loan with an LTV ratio that equals or exceeds 90 percent at origination, the bank should require appropriate credit enhancement in the form of either mortgage insurance or readily marketable collateral.

In establishing internal LTV limits, the bank should carefully consider the bank-specific and market factors listed in the "Loan Portfolio Management Considerations" section of this booklet, as well as any other relevant risk factors, such as the particular subcategory or type of loan. If the bank identifies greater risk for a particular subcategory of loans within an overall category, the internal LTV limit for that subcategory may be lower than the limit established for the overall category.

The LTV ratio is only one of several important credit factors to be considered when underwriting a real estate loan. Other credit factors to be taken into account are discussed in the "Underwriting Standards" section of this booklet. Because of these other factors, the establishment of these supervisory limits should not be interpreted to mean that loans underwritten to these limits are automatically considered sound.

LTV is calculated by dividing the loan amount by the market value of the property securing the loan plus the amount of any readily marketable collateral and other acceptable collateral[6] that secures the loan. The total amount of all senior liens on or interests in such property should be included.

Standby letters of credit secured by the property that are issued to governmental authorities to ensure the completion of certain improvements, the cost of which are to be funded by the loan, need not be included in the loan amount for the purpose of calculating the SLTV. When the cost of the improvements is to be funded from other sources, however, the standby letter of credit should be included.

The value used in calculating the SLTV can be as-is, the prospective market value as completed ("as-completed") or prospective market value as stabilized ("as-stabilized"). An as-is value would be appropriate for calculating the SLTV for raw land or stabilized properties. For an owner-occupied building or a property to be constructed that is preleased, the as-completed value should generally be used. An as-stabilized value would be appropriate for an existing property that is not stabilized or a property to be constructed that is not preleased to stabilized levels. For a further discussion of as-completed and as-stabilized values, see the "prospective market value" entry in this booklet's glossary.

The following sections provide additional guidance in determining the appropriate SLTV.

Applying SLTV Limits to Loans Financing Various Stages of Development

SLTV limits should be applied to the underlying property that collateralizes the loan. For loans that fund multiple stages of the same real estate project (for example, a loan for land acquisition, land development, and construction of an office building), the appropriate LTV limit for the completed project is the limit applicable to the final stage of the project funded by the loan. Total disbursements for each element of the development, however, are subject to its particular SLTV limits. This can be illustrated by considering the various development stages.

---

[6] "Other acceptable collateral" means any collateral in which the lender has a perfected security interest that has a quantifiable value and is accepted by the lender in accordance with safe and sound lending practices. Other acceptable collateral should be appropriately discounted by the lender consistent with the lender's usual practices for making loans secured by such collateral. Other acceptable collateral includes unconditional irrevocable standby letters of credit for the benefit of the lender.

A land development loan is defined in 12 CFR 34, subpart D (national banks), and 12 CFR 160.101 (federal savings associations), as "an extension of credit for the purpose of improving unimproved real property before the erection of structures. The improvement of unimproved real property may include the laying or placement of sewers, water pipes, utility cables, streets, and other infrastructure necessary for future development." Finished lot loans and buildable lot loans are synonymous with land development loans. The SLTV ratio for a land development loan, a finished lot loan, or a buildable lot loan is 75 percent. The LTV may not exceed 75 percent until construction of a permanent building commences.

The bank may use the higher appropriate LTV ratio when actual construction begins on the next stage of development. For example, the bank may advance 65 percent for raw land and up to 75 percent when converting the raw land into finished lots. The bank may advance up to 80 percent of the appraised market value when construction of a permanent commercial, multifamily or other nonresidential building commences or up to 85 percent when construction of one- to four-family residences commences.

If the bank commits to finance only one phase of development or construction rather than an entire multi-phase tract development project, the loan amount is the legally binding commitment for that stage for purposes of calculating LTV.

Disbursements should not exceed actual development or construction outlays while ensuring that the borrower maintains appropriate levels of hard equity throughout the term of the loan as discussed in the "Underwriting Standards" section of this booklet.

Calculating SLTV for Loan Financing Tract Development

For residential tract developments, the loan amount is the total amount of a loan, line of credit, or other legally binding commitment. For a line of credit, the legally binding commitment amount is based on the term of the credit agreement. For facilities that utilize a borrowing base formula to determine the funds available to the borrower, the loan amount is the bank's legally binding commitment (that is, the outstanding balance of the facility plus any availability under the borrowing base). Value is the lesser of the borrower's actual development or construction costs or the prospective market value of completed units securing the loan multiplied by their percentage of completion.

The value of the real estate collateral for the calculation of the LTV ratio is the market value as defined in the interagency appraisal regulations (refer to the glossary for the definition of market value). The appraisal should reflect a market value upon completion of construction of the home(s) and the market value of any other collateral, such as lots or undeveloped land. Further, the appraisal must consider an analysis of appropriate deductions and discounts for unsold units, including holding costs, marketing costs, and entrepreneurial profit. For loans to purchase land or existing lots, "value" means the lesser of the actual acquisition cost or the current market value.

The bank should calculate the LTV ratio at the time of loan origination and recalculate the ratio whenever collateral is released or substituted. If the LTV ratio exceeds the SLTV limits, the bank should comply with guidelines for loans exceeding the SLTV limits.

Calculating SLTV for Loan Collateralized by Two or More Properties

If a loan is cross-collateralized by two or more properties or is secured by a collateral pool of two or more properties, the appropriate maximum loan amount under SLTV limits is the sum of the market value of each property, less senior liens, multiplied by the appropriate LTV limit for each property.

This calculation is performed by multiplying each property's market value by the appropriate SLTV ratio, then deducting any existing senior liens associated with the property, and lastly adding the individual results. If the total equals or exceeds the loan amount, the loan conforms to the supervisory limits. If the results are less than the loan amount, the loan does not conform to the SLTV limits.

As shown in the following example, if a collateral pool comprises raw land valued at $75,000 (subject to a $25,000 prior lien) and an improved commercial property valued at $250,000 (subject to a $125,000 prior lien), the maximum total aggregate amount that could be loaned against the collateral pool while conforming to the SLTV limit is $111,250.

($75,000 x 65%) – $25,000	=	$ 23,750
($250,000 x 85%) – $125,000	=	87,500
		$ 111,250

To ensure that collateral margins remain within the SLTV limits, the bank should recalculate the loan's LTV for conformity with these limits whenever collateral substitutions are made to or collateral is released from the collateral pool.

Loans Exceeding SLTV Ratio Limits

The interagency guidelines recognize that appropriate LTV limits vary not only among categories of real estate loans but also among individual loans. Therefore, it may be appropriate in individual cases for the bank to originate or purchase loans with LTV ratios in excess of the SLTV limits, based on the support provided by other credit factors.

The aggregate amount, or basket, of all loans in excess of the SLTV limits at origination should not exceed 100 percent of total capital, as defined in 12 CFR 3.2(e) (national banks) or 12 CFR 167.5(c) (federal savings associations). Loans that met SLTV limits at origination for which the collateral subsequently declined in value do not constitute SLTV exceptions and are not included in the calculation of the aggregate amount.

Within that aggregate limit, total loans to finance commercial, agricultural, multifamily, or other non-one- to four-family residential properties should not exceed 30 percent of total capital. This segment is often referred to as the commercial basket and includes

- raw land with an LTV ratio greater than 65 percent.
- commercial land development with an LTV ratio greater than 75 percent.
- commercial, multifamily, and other nonresidential construction with an LTV ratio greater than 80 percent.
- improved property with an LTV ratio greater than 85 percent.

The remainder of the total basket (up to 100 percent) is available for all categories of nonconforming loans on one- to four-family residential property, including

- raw land zoned for development with an LTV ratio greater than 65 percent.
- land development loans with an LTV ratio greater than 75 percent.
- construction loans with an LTV ratio greater than 85 percent.
- loans on non-owner-occupied property with an LTV ratio greater than 85 percent.
- permanent mortgages and home-equity loans on owner-occupied property equal to or exceeding 90 percent LTV, without mortgage insurance, readily marketable collateral or other acceptable collateral.

For a loan exceeding SLTV limits, the entire outstanding balance should be included in the nonconforming basket, not just the portion exceeding the limit. If the bank holds a first and second lien on a parcel of real estate and the combined commitment exceeds the appropriate SLTV limit, both loans should be reported in the bank's nonconforming loan totals. Further, the bank should include loans secured by the same property if any one of those loans exceeds the SLTV limits, and any recourse obligation of any such loan sold with recourse. A loan need no longer be reported to the board of directors as part of aggregate totals when reduction in principal or senior liens, or additional contribution of collateral or equity (e.g., improvements to the real property securing the loan), brings the LTV into compliance with SLTV limits.

Excluded Transactions

The guidelines recognize that there are a number of lending situations in which certain factors may outweigh the need to apply the SLTV limits. These include

- loans guaranteed or insured by the U.S. government or its agencies, provided that the amount of the guaranty or insurance is at least equal to the portion of the loan that exceeds the SLTV limit.
- loans or portions of loans backed by the full faith and credit of a state government, provided that the amount of the assurance is at least equal to the portion of the loan that exceeds the SLTV limit.
- loans guaranteed or insured by a state, municipal, or local government, or an agency thereof, provided that the amount of the guaranty or insurance is at least equal to the portion of the loan that exceeds the SLTV limit, and provided that the bank has determined that the guarantor or insurer has the financial capacity and willingness to perform under the terms of the guaranty or insurance agreement.
- loans that are to be sold promptly after origination, without recourse, to a financially responsible third party.

- loans that are renewed, refinanced, or restructured without the advancement of new funds or an increase in the line of credit (except for reasonable closing costs), or loans that are renewed, refinanced, or restructured in connection with a loan workout with or without the advancement of new funds, where consistent with safe and sound banking practices and part of a clearly defined and well-documented program to achieve orderly liquidation of the debt, reduce risk of loss, or maximize recovery on the loan.
- loans that facilitate the sale of real estate acquired by the bank in the ordinary course of collecting a debt previously contracted in good faith.
- loans for which the bank takes a lien on or interest in real property as additional collateral through an abundance of caution. For example, an abundance of caution exists when the bank takes a blanket lien on all or substantially all of the assets of the borrower, and the value of the real property is low relative to the aggregate value of all other collateral. When the real estate is the only form of collateral, this exclusion would not apply.
- loans, such as working capital loans, in which the bank does not rely principally on real estate as security and the extension of credit is not used to acquire, develop, or construct improvement on real property.
- loans for the purpose of financing permanent improvements to real property, but not secured by the property, if such security interest is not required by prudent underwriting practice.

Exceptions to General Lending Policy

The lending policy should include procedures for considering loans that are exceptions to the bank's lending policy. These procedures should include the bank's approval process, the appropriate level of management approval required for each type or size of lending transaction, and requirements for reporting exceptions to the board of directors or a designated committee thereof.

Supervisory Review of Real Estate Lending Policies and Practices

Examiners should review the bank's policies and practices to determine whether the bank's real estate lending program is consistent with safe and sound banking practices, satisfies the requirements of the "Real Estate Lending Standards" in subpart D of 12 CFR 34 (national banks) or 12 CFR 160.101 (federal savings associations), and reflects an appropriate consideration of the "Interagency Guidelines for Real Estate Lending Policies" contained in appendix A to subpart D of part 34 (national banks) and the appendix to 12 CFR 160.101 (federal savings associations).

When evaluating the adequacy of real estate lending policies and practices, examiners should consider the

- nature and scope of the bank's real estate lending activities.
- size and financial condition of the bank.
- quality of management and internal controls.

- expertise and size of the lending and loan administration staff.
- market conditions.

Examiners should determine whether the bank monitors compliance with its real estate lending policy. Examiners also should review lending policy exception reports to assess the frequency and nature of policy exceptions and to determine whether exceptions to loan policy are adequately documented, reported, and appropriate in light of all of the relevant credit considerations. An excessive number of exceptions to the real estate lending policy could indicate that the bank is unduly relaxing its underwriting practices or may suggest that the bank needs to revise its loan policy.

Acquisition, Development, and Construction Lending

In its simplest form, ADC lending may finance the land acquisition, land preparation, and construction of a single residential or commercial building. Often, however, ADC lending finances a single- or multiple-phase development of many units. ADC is highly specialized lending that requires a thorough understanding of its inherent risks. This section discusses the underwriting, policies, and controls that are necessary for prudent ADC lending.

ADC lending presents unique risks not encountered in the term financing of existing real estate. Assessing performance on a development or construction loan can be challenging because most are underwritten without required amortization or project-generated interest payments. Absent such objective performance measures, examiners must fully evaluate the projected cash flow of the project, compare actual progress to the initial plan, and when applicable, analyze guarantor support. This analysis must consider the feasibility of the project, given current conditions, planned construction, and the level of fully funded debt.

Types of ADC Lending

While ADC lending can take various forms, the following are the most commonly encountered ones.

Unsecured Working Capital Loans to Finance Real Estate

A developer may wish to borrow on an unsecured basis, often in the form of a line of credit, to acquire a building site, eliminate title impediments, pay architect or commitment fees, or meet minimum working capital requirements established by other construction lenders. Repayment of an unsecured front-money loan may come from the first draw against a construction loan. The bank extending such an unsecured loan should require the construction loan agreement to permit repayment of the working capital loan on the first draw.

As with other unsecured credit, it is critical that the bank identify adequate sources of repayment and intended timing of repayment. Banks should avoid making these loans to an illiquid or highly leveraged borrower or where the source of repayment is dependent on assets in which the bank has no collateral interest.

Because such loans are inherently risky, the bank should ensure that it has the necessary expertise to evaluate and manage the risk before engaging in this type of lending. Banks should avoid extending unsecured working capital loans to fund a developer's equity investment in a project or to cover cost overruns, as overruns may be indicative of an undercapitalized project or an inexperienced or unskilled developer.

Land Acquisition Loans

Land acquisition loans finance the acquisition of undeveloped land. These loans are often made in conjunction with land or lot development and construction loans. In some cases, these loans may be made for speculative purposes without plans to immediately develop the property. Such loans are among the riskiest types of real estate loans. Undeveloped land generates no cash flow in most cases and requires other sources of cash to service the debt. Banks that finance land with no immediate and well-defined development plans should carefully analyze the borrower's or guarantor's ability to service the debt and the plans for repayment. Land loans made for speculative purposes should require considerable equity and be extended infrequently.

Land Development Loans

Land development loans fund the preparation of land for construction. This may include infrastructure improvements required for future development, such as sewer and water pipes, utility cables, grading, and street construction. Often, acquisition and development loans are extended together to finance both the acquisition and development of land.

Tract Development Loans

A tract development is a project with five or more units that is constructed as a single development. A unit may refer to a residential building lot, a detached single-family home, an attached single-family home, or a residence in a condominium building. Tract developments may include other multiple-unit developments, such as office or industrial parks. In addition to the site improvements previously cited, these loans may finance construction of common amenities or infrastructure, such as clubhouses and recreational facilities. The source of repayment for these loans may be proceeds from the sale of lots to other developers or from the proceeds of a construction facility extended to the original developer to finance construction of for-sale or for-lease units. Repayment of these loans is discussed further in the "ADC Loan Structure" section of this booklet.

Construction Loans for Commercial Properties

Commercial construction loans finance the construction or renovation of non-one- to four-family properties for owner occupancy, lease, or sale. This can encompass a wide variety of property types and projects, including apartments, office buildings, retail centers, hotels, and industrial and mixed-use developments.

A bank must consider the source and timing of the repayment of construction financing as part of its underwriting process and determine whether the projected net operating income (NOI) of the completed project supports the expected value upon completion. A definition of NOI can be found in the glossary of this booklet.

Loans to Finance Repositioning or Rehabilitation

In addition to new construction, a bank might finance the acquisition of an underperforming property in which the borrower intends to improve the property's performance, typically by performing physical upgrades or curing deferred maintenance and improving the management. While this can present an opportunity for the borrower to enhance a property's value in many cases, the bank must closely examine the borrower's assumptions to determine the likelihood that the projections can be realized. The bank should carefully scrutinize the borrower's ability to achieve his or her objectives. An evaluation of the borrower's track record with similar properties should be a critical consideration.

Banks may also finance an older property's rehabilitation, modernization, or conversion to another use that may involve extensive improvements or modifications. In such cases, the bank must carefully examine the construction budget and should obtain an independent evaluation of the budget's adequacy from a qualified engineer or architect. It can be more difficult to accurately estimate the costs of these kinds of projects than of new construction due to unobservable conditions.

Bridge Loans

Banks may provide short-term financing to allow newly constructed or acquired commercial properties to reach stabilization. Bridge loans are usually written for a period of up to three years and allow for the lease-up and income stabilization necessary to enable either sale or qualification for permanent financing. Income and value assumptions should be well supported and carefully analyzed by the bank.

Permanent Loan Commitments

While not a type of ADC loan, commitments for permanent financing sometimes play an important role in ADC financing. Permanent loans, also referred to as "take-outs," are term loans that replace construction loans. Permanent financing may be provided by either the construction lender or another lender. In addition to banks, permanent financing is often provided by life insurance companies and pension funds, and through commercial mortgage-backed securitizations.

Commitments for take-out financing may be provided before or after construction completion and lease-up. Commitments issued before completion and lease-up usually fall into one of two categories: stand-by commitments and forward commitments.

A stand-by commitment provides back-up financing should other permanent financing not be found. Fees are usually required at commitment with additional fees due if the commitment is funded. The fee structure and interest rate may often be intended to dissuade the borrower from exercising the commitment and to encourage him or her to find other sources of funding. Borrowers may sometimes obtain stand-by commitments to fulfill a construction lender's requirement for a committed take-out. Construction lenders who rely on stand-by commitments should carefully review the terms of the commitment and the likelihood that the project will meet the criteria for funding. Lenders should also thoroughly investigate the willingness and ability of the issuer to fund.

A forward commitment for permanent financing provides a commitment to refinance a construction loan upon future completion and, almost always, lease-up. Forward commitments allow a permanent lender to originate the loan earlier in the development process and usually provide the borrower the ability to lock in a fixed rate in advance of funding. These commitments tend to be more prevalent when competition for loans among permanent lenders is high and in greater demand among borrowers in periods of rising interest rates. As with stand-by commitments, the willingness and ability of the lender to fund and the conditions for funding should be carefully considered.

While construction lenders sometimes take comfort in stand-by or forward commitments, these commitments may mitigate little of the risk assumed by the lender in making the construction loan. Although these commitments can provide interest rate protection and some indication that the project meets permanent-market criteria, they require the completion of construction and, in most cases, are subject to performance criteria such as lease-up to breakeven or better with leases at minimum rental rates.

A bank should evaluate a construction project and make its credit decision recognizing the risk that the take-out commitment may not fund.

Construction Issues

Construction loans finance the creation of collateral and their repayment is dependent on the collateral's completion. These are a few of the factors that can pose threats to successful completion.

- Fraudulent diversion of construction draws.
- Liens filed by contractors, subcontractors, or material suppliers for nonpayment.
- Delays caused by labor disputes or failure of major suppliers to deliver materials.
- Failure of the contractor or a subcontractor to complete construction or complete to specifications. This may be due to inadequate experience, negligence, or financial failure.
- Cost overruns due to unforeseen conditions, such as inaccurate budgets; increases in materials or transportation expense; material or labor shortages; increased interest expense; inadequate soil or other subsurface conditions; or delays caused by inclement weather.
- Loan administration errors.

While many of these risks are beyond the control of the bank, some can be mitigated by (1) careful scrutiny of the plans and budget; (2) frequent and routine inspections; (3) thoroughly investigating the financial condition and reputation of the borrower, contractor, and subcontractors; and (4) utilizing effective loan administration procedures.

The use of performance and payment bonds and title insurance can further mitigate this risk. A payment bond mitigates the risk of priority liens being recorded by insuring the payment of subcontractors and material suppliers. A performance bond insures the completion of the project by the subcontractor. The bank's policy should require bonds for all projects of a material size where the borrower and contractor are separate entities (a contractor related to the borrower cannot generally be bonded). Title insurance can protect the lender from losses due to fraud and construction liens.

The bank can mitigate the risk of cost overruns by requiring the borrower to enter into a fixed-price contract with the contractor. If the borrower and the contractor are the same or are related, the contract should specify cost plus a fee with a guaranteed maximum price. Regardless of whether the borrower employs a third-party contractor or the borrower acts as the contractor, the bank should take care to ensure that the contractor has sufficient expertise and financial capacity.

Market Conditions

Construction lending activities are particularly sensitive to market conditions. For this reason, a thorough market analysis is a critical component of the underwriting process.

For properties under construction, demand from prospective tenants or purchasers may erode after construction begins because of a general economic slowdown or an increase in the supply of competing properties. If actual rental rates achieved during lease-up are lower than those projected, a project's viability can be threatened by a failure to generate income sufficient to support its debt and the expected collateral value. A decline in demand or increase in the supply of for-sale properties can threaten full principal repayment.

Prudent loan policies seek to mitigate market risk by establishing minimum levels of preleasing or sales as a condition of commitment or funding. Experience has shown, however, that presales may not be a reliable indicator of actual future sales because these purchase commitments may not result in sales if values decline. Banks should carefully analyze and monitor presales and preleasing, ensuring that they represent bona fide commitments and that deposits have been collected and are meaningful.

Construction Lending Policies, Procedures, and Internal Controls

Banks are expected to establish and implement sound policies, procedures, and internal controls to support ADC lending activities. Although policies should address the different types of construction lending undertaken by the bank, the following elements should be included as part of a sound construction lending program. More specific considerations for these elements are discussed in other parts of this booklet.

Acceptable loan types and limits: Policies should define acceptable types of construction loans and construction lending concentration limits that are consistent with the board's appetite for risk. Banks should consider establishing sub-limits, defined by property type, geographic market, and other relevant factors where appropriate.

Sound analysis and underwriting: Banks that participate in any phase of construction lending should maintain sound analysis and underwriting processes to evaluate the quality of loan opportunities and help mitigate risk. Feasibility analyses, reviews of construction and site plans, construction budgets, as well as borrowers, contractors, and subcontractors are important to identifying and understanding the risk inherent in construction loan proposals.

Minimum standards of documentation: The bank's construction program should establish minimum standards of documentation consistent with the type of construction lending performed.

Construction loan administration: Banks that finance construction are expected to maintain sound loan administration and monitoring programs. Timely construction monitoring is essential to evaluating construction progress, ensuring disbursement requests are appropriate, alerting the bank to potential problems (such as significant cost overruns or project delays), and ensuring that sales proceeds are applied to principal in a manner consistent with the loan agreement. Architect or engineering inspection reports, independent of the borrower, should be required with each draw to ensure work is done according to specification. A representative of the lender should at least occasionally inspect the site to ensure work is completed as reported. Inspection reports should state compliance with plans and specifications, support disbursements, and state whether or not the project is progressing as anticipated.

Disbursement controls: Disbursement controls are an important element of construction risk management. Banks should ensure that construction draws are commensurate with verified improvements and that the budget remains in balance with sufficient funds available to fund completion.

Evaluating the Developer Borrower

Because the expected value of the project is not realized until the project is completed, the bank should assess the borrower's ability to complete the project within budget, on time, and according to the construction plans.

Before issuing a commitment to finance proposed construction, the bank should analyze and document the borrower's background, including reputation and experience, to determine the project's likelihood of success. This should include a review of the contractor's and major subcontractors' ability to successfully complete the type of project to be undertaken.

The bank should also perform a careful analysis of the borrower's financial condition to ensure that the borrower has sufficient financial capacity to ensure completion. This is discussed in the "Analysis of Borrower's and Guarantor's Financial Condition" section of this booklet.

Determining Project Feasibility

The bank's analysis should include a determination of the project's feasibility. Feasibility describes the likelihood that the project as proposed will be economically successful. Feasibility studies can be included as part of an independent appraisal or as a separate analysis. Banks should understand that feasibility studies commissioned by the borrower may be biased and should be critically reviewed. While studies and appraisals can be helpful in providing useful information and analysis, the bank should conduct its own analysis of the project. This section discusses analyses important to determining a project's feasibility.

Plans and Budget

The construction budget, along with the project pro forma, is one of the most critical elements in determining project feasibility. The developer should provide a detailed line-item budget that should be carefully reviewed by a qualified individual to determine if the budget is appropriate and reasonable.

Construction budgets typically categorize costs as hard and soft costs. Hard costs generally include on- or off-site improvements, building construction and other reasonable and customary costs paid to construct or improve a project, including general contractor's fees and other expenses normally included in a construction contract such as bonding and contractor insurance. Soft costs include interest and other development costs such as fees and related predevelopment expenses. The budget should include a contingency account to fund unanticipated overruns. Project costs payable to related parties such as developer fees, leasing expenses, brokerage commissions, and management fees may be included in the soft costs provided the costs are reasonable in comparison to the cost of similar services from third parties. Interest or preferred returns payable to equity partners or subordinated debt holders should not be included in the construction budget. Other items that should not be included in the budget are the developer's general corporate overhead and selling costs that are to be funded out of sales proceeds such as brokerage commissions and other closing costs.

The budget should be reviewed to determine if it realistically reflects the cost to construct the improvements in accordance with the plans and whether the improvements are sufficiently functional and compare favorably with competitive properties in its market. Banks should be wary of budgets that lack detail or appear to be overly optimistic. An inaccurate budget can lead to cost overruns and a need to advance additional funds for completion. Rarely does an increase in cost result in an increase in value.

The economic purpose of developing a property is to create value over and above the project's cost. This difference between the prospective value and cost to construct is the developer's profit. This profit is the incentive required by a developer to assume the risk of construction and sale or lease-up and varies depending on the development's complexity and risk; a development that does not create this incentive (prospective value is not sufficiently higher than its cost) is generally not feasible. Furthermore, a project budget with modest or no developer profit leaves inadequate room for cost overruns. Additionally, if the bank must take possession of an incomplete project, the lack of profit available to a prospective purchaser for completion complicates the bank's efforts to dispose of the property in its incomplete state and may require completion by the bank or its sale at a price that may result in a loss.

The developer's profit should generally be funded only by sales, by construction loan funds only upon construction completion and lease-up, or by subsequent term financing. Profit contributes to collateral value only to the degree that the project is successful. Funding a developer's profit for an incomplete project diminishes his or her incentive to complete and lease or sell the units in a real estate project and has led to problems for lenders.

A developer fee (not to be confused with profit) is often included in the project budget. This fee represents compensation for the management of the project and the developer's overhead directly incurred for that project only. In practice, its disbursement may be either deferred or disbursed based on the percentage of the project's completion. This fee varies but typically does not exceed 4 percent of the project cost.

The bank's policy should establish loan limits as a maximum percentage of cost as well as value to ensure sufficient borrower equity. Equity is important in ensuring the borrower continues to have an economic interest in the success of the property and provides a cushion for cost overruns and leasing or sales shortfalls. The bank's lending policy should clearly state the requirements for borrower equity such as specifying the amounts required, the acceptable types of equity and sources, and the timing of its contribution.

The bank's policy should require that equity be contributed before disbursements of the construction loan commence. When the injection of any equity is deferred for contribution at a later point in the development process, the bank should be assured that this equity is, and will remain, available. Allowing the deferred contribution of equity can significantly increase completion risk and should not be allowed routinely or in the absence of compelling mitigating factors.

Acceptable equity usually includes actual cash expended by a developer for the purchase of a site and initial costs paid, such as engineering or permits related directly to the project. Deferred developer's profit, incurred overhead expenses, or interest or other holding fees paid or accrued on contributed land should not be considered equity.

Sufficient funds should be available at all times to ensure the completion of the project. It is a weak practice to approve a loan to finance only partial construction of a project with the expectation that the remaining funds will be found elsewhere. Exceptions to this may be financing for later phases of phased developments or loans that finance the development of lots but where unit construction financing is expected to be provided by other lenders.

Pro Forma Financial Statements

A credible pro forma is a key determinant of a project's feasibility. The bank should carefully review the pro forma statement to determine whether the underlying assumptions and related projections are reasonable based on the bank's knowledge of the market and income and expenses for similar properties.

Regardless of the cost to construct a property, the value of an income-producing property is dependent to a great degree on the expected NOI. For this reason, expected costs and the value supported by the NOI must be considered together. Construction costs that closely approach or exceed the expected value of the project's income generally indicate that a project is not feasible for reasons discussed under the "Plans and Budget" section of this booklet.

For projects that involve unit sales, the bank should analyze the timing of expected cash inflows from loan and sales proceeds along with cash outflows for development costs to ensure that sufficient cash is available throughout the development period.

Site Analysis

This analysis helps determine the site's suitability for the proposed development. Consideration should be given to the project type, location, ingress and egress, physical dimensions, current use of the property, location, topology, easements, availability of public utilities, zoning, and development costs.

Demographic Analysis

Demographics should be evaluated to determine the likelihood of the project's immediate and longer term success. Is household formation growing? Do income levels in the property's market area support the rent projections in the case of residential rental properties? The U.S. Census Bureau can be a useful source of demographic information.

Market Analysis

The market analysis should review the supply and demand characteristics and project desirability, and should consider existing and anticipated comparable properties. This may include an analysis of effective rental rates, sales prices, vacancy rates, building starts, and absorption. The analysis should consider the amenities and physical characteristics of the subject property and compare them with those of competitive properties. The results of this review should support the revenue assumptions relied on in the pro forma financial statements.

While supply considerations are always important for real estate, they are especially critical in the evaluation of a construction project. As with any other product, an increase in demand spurs an increase in production and, in turn, an increase in supply. Unlike many other products, however, real estate has a long production cycle. While properties may be built for sale or lease to a purchaser or tenant that has already been identified, properties—or a portion of them—are often built on a speculative basis. Because of the length of the development and construction process, speculatively developed properties must meet demand that exists at a point in the future rather than the demand that exists when development begins.

To evaluate future demand and supply, it is important to have an understanding of the current and planned development activity in the local market. Information on local building permits and construction starts is usually available from data services or directly from local government offices. Projecting the level of future supply can be difficult and cannot accurately account for future permits and construction that may begin after development of the property has commenced. Because of this, supply often overshoots the expected demand resulting in prolonged lease up and sales periods and declines in rental rates and sales prices.

Collateral Valuation for ADC Loans

Appraisals used to support construction loans must include the current market value of the property (often referred to as the "as is" value of the property), which reflects the property's actual physical condition, use, and zoning designation as of a current effective date of the appraisal. If the highest and best use of the property is for redevelopment to a different use, the cost of demolition and site preparation should be considered in the analysis. OCC Bulletin 2005-32, "Frequently Asked Questions: Residential Tract Development Lending," provides guidance in the valuation of collateral for ADC loans.

The construction loan appraisal must also include a prospective market value. The prospective market value upon completion ("as-complete") is an estimate of the property's market value as of the time that development is expected to be completed. A prospective market value upon stabilization ("as-stabilized") is an estimate of the property's market value as of the date the property is projected to achieve stabilized occupancy. Stabilized occupancy is the occupancy level that a property is expected to achieve after the property is exposed to the market for lease over a reasonable period of time and at comparable terms and conditions to other similar properties.

Market values for proposed construction or renovation, partially leased or vacant buildings, non-market lease terms, and tract developments with unsold units must analyze and report appropriate deductions and discounts.

Appraisals of Tract Developments

As with all appraisals, an appraisal for a residential tract development must meet the minimum appraisal standards in the appraisal regulations and guidelines. Appraisals for these properties must reflect deductions and discounts for holding costs, marketing costs, and entrepreneurial profit. In some limited circumstances, the bank may rely on appraisals of the individual units to meet the agencies' appraisal requirements and to determine market value for calculating the LTV ratio.

The bank can exclude presold units to determine whether an appraisal of a tract development is required. A unit may be considered presold if a buyer has entered into a binding contract to purchase the unit and has made a substantial and nonrefundable earnest money deposit. The bank should obtain sufficient documentation to determine that the buyer has entered into a legally binding sales contract and has obtained a written prequalification or commitment for permanent financing.

When the bank finances raw land, lot development, or lot acquisition as part of a residential tract development, the bank must obtain an appraisal of the entire tract of raw land or all lots that includes appropriate deductions and discounts. The appraisal should reflect the "as-is" market value of the property in its current condition and existing zoning as well as the prospective market value of the land upon completion of land improvements, if applicable. The land improvements may include the construction of utilities, streets, and other infrastructure necessary for future development. An appraisal of raw land to be valued as developed lots should reflect a reasonable time frame during which development occurs. The feasibility study or the market analysis in the appraisal should support the absorption period for the developed lots; otherwise, a portion of the tract development should be valued as raw land and factored into the discounting process.

Appraisals of Residential Models

For residential models, the bank ordinarily obtains an appraisal for each model or floor plan that a borrower is planning to build and offer for sale. The model appraisal typically includes the value of a base lot in a particular development without consideration to the costs of, or value attributed to, specific options, upgrades, or lot premiums.

If the bank finances the construction of a residential tract development, an appraisal of the model(s) provides relevant information for the appraiser to consider in providing a market value of the development. That is, the value attributable to the models is used as a basis for estimating a market value for the tract development by reflecting the mix of units and adjusting for options, upgrades, and lot premiums. The market value should also reflect an analysis of appropriate deductions and discounts for holding costs, marketing costs, and entrepreneurial profit.

For construction of units that are not part of a tract development, a model's appraisal may be used to estimate the market value of the individual home, if the model and base lot are substantially the same as the subject home and the appraisal meets the agencies' appraisal requirements and is still valid. In assessing the appraisal's validity, the bank should consider the passage of time and current market conditions.[7] When underwriting a loan to finance construction of a single home, the bank should consider the value of the particular lot and any options and upgrades relative to the values in the appraisal of the model.

---

[7] See the "Appraisals and Evaluations" section of this booklet for a detailed discussion of the criteria for determining the validity of an appraisal or evaluation.

When an Appraisal Might Not Require Deductions and Discounts

An appraisal of a tract development must analyze and report appropriate deductions and discounts. The bank review of the appraisal report should include an analysis of these deductions and discounts.

There are limited circumstances, however, when the structure of a proposed loan mitigates the need to obtain a tract development appraisal. If all of the units to be developed can be built and sold within a 12-month period, no discounting is required and the bank may use appraisals of the individual units to satisfy the agencies' appraisal requirements and as a basis for computing the LTV ratio. The bank should be able to demonstrate, through a feasibility study or market analysis conducted independently of the borrower and the bank, that all units collateralizing the loan are expected to be constructed and sold within 12 months. For LTV purposes, the "value" in this isolated case is the lower of the sum of the individual appraised values of the units ("sum of the retail sellout values") or the borrower's actual development and construction costs. The borrower should maintain appropriate levels of hard equity (for example, cash or unencumbered investment in the underlying property) throughout the construction and marketing periods.

If the bank finances a unit's construction under a revolving line of credit in which a borrowing base sets the availability of funds, the bank may be able to use appraisals on the individual units to satisfy the agencies' appraisal requirements and as a basis for computing the LTV ratio. This is the case if the bank limits the number of construction starts and completed, unsold homes included in the borrowing base and if the bank satisfies the conditions described in the preceding paragraph. If the borrowing base includes developed lots or raw land to be developed into lots, the appraisal obtained by the bank must reflect appropriate deductions and discounts.

Appraisal Requirements for Construction of Condominiums

For a condominium building with five or more units, the bank must obtain an appraisal of the building that reflects appropriate deductions and discounts for holding costs, marketing costs, and entrepreneurial profit. The bank may not use the aggregate retail sales prices of the individual units as the market value to calculate the LTV ratio. For purposes of this booklet, condominium buildings are distinguished from other types of residential properties if construction of the entire building has to be completed before any one unit is occupied.

If the bank finances the construction of a single condominium building with fewer than five units, the bank may be able to rely on appraisals of the individual units to satisfy the regulatory appraisal requirements and to determine the market value for calculating the LTV ratio.

Further information on appraisal requirements can be found in OCC Bulletin 2010-42, "Sound Practices for Appraisals and Evaluations: Interagency Appraisal and Evaluation Guidelines." The guidelines provide an expanded discussion of the requirements for deductions and discounts in a discounted cash-flow analysis.

ADC Loan Structure

The bank's lending policy should define acceptable tenors for various types of construction loans. The tenor should consider the time needed for construction and stabilization or sale. The tenor should not be shorter than that required for completion. The bank may wish to provide construction financing that covers the expected construction period with the facility converting to bridge financing for the expected stabilization period.

Appropriate terms of repayment are critical when financing multiple-unit developments. Multiple-unit ADC financing is usually provided by separate development and construction facilities with lot repayment for the development loan being made from the first draw of the construction loan. A prudent development and construction loan policy includes requirements for principal curtailments to ensure periodic re-margining if sales or sales prices fall short of projections. The bank should satisfy itself of the borrower's or guarantor's ability to meet any curtailment requirements.

Typically, the construction loan agreement permits a limited number of speculative units and models, allowing the builder to have units available for marketing and sale while permitting the bank to better manage risk. The bank should carefully consider the expected absorption rate when establishing limits on the construction of speculative units.

Construction loans that finance multiple units or phases must be structured to ensure that repayment appropriately follows unit sales; adequate pay downs must be made as the collateral is sold and released. For multiple-unit developments, full repayment should be required before the sale of all units. To accomplish this, the amount that the bank would require to release its unit lien (the release price) would be some multiple of the lot's proportional share of the total value of all the units. This is commonly referred to as "acceleration."

For example, assume a developer is developing 100 single-family lots projected to sell on average for $30,000 each. Also assume that the project was appraised for $2 million, reflecting the discounted net cash flows from the lot sales. The bank agrees to lend $1.5 million (75 percent of the appraised value of the project) and wants to be fully paid with the sales of 80 percent, or 80, of the lots.

To be fully paid with the sale of the 80th lot, the construction loan agreement would specify a release price of 125 percent (100/80). If the lots were equal in value, the release price would be calculated as follows: $1,500,000/100 = $15,000 x 125% = $18,750. Alternatively, if the bank wishes to be paid out over the sale of 75 percent of the lots, the release price would be 134 percent (100/75 rounded up) of the proportionate debt or $15,000 x 134% = $20,100. When values among lots differ, separate release prices can be established for each lot. A development that generates little developer profit on the lots, i.e., the sales price is not sufficiently greater than the cost, will have difficulty paying off lots on an accelerated basis.

For multiple-unit loans, such as those for lot development or condominiums, the maximum number of units that may be financed should consider the tenor and anticipated rate of unit sales. For example, if the maximum term is 24 months, units are expected to be absorbed at an average rate of 10 per quarter, the bank wishes to be paid off after the sale of 80 percent of the units (acceleration of 1.25), and it is expected to take six months for units to be available for sale, the maximum number of units that could be financed, given the maximum 24-month tenor, would be ((24-6)/3) x 10 x 1.25 = 75 units. This may also be used to determine the required tenor to finance a given number of units.

Banks may wish to finance larger tract developments in phases to better control risk. A prudent practice is to finance each phase with separate loans or sub-limits with the funding of subsequent phases dependent on the performance of the previous phase. Financing development in phases may require the construction of amenities such as clubhouses and recreational facilities or site improvements that benefit all phases even though their cost is funded with the first phase. The bank should apply a portion of the unit release prices to pay down the loan amount associated with these common improvements using a method similar to the one described above with an emphasis on proceeds from the earlier units where possible. This may be best accomplished by providing a separate facility for the common improvements. This method can also be used to repay a facility that finances models.

Appropriate covenants for construction or development loans may include

- a limit on the permissible number of speculative units and models for the subject property.
- a limit on the number or dollar amount of unsold units including speculative units and models a builder may have for all projects at any one time, and for projects financed by the bank.
- a limit on raw land inventory or the number of attached projects in progress at any one time.
- limits on additional debts, guarantees, and liens.
- the borrower's or guarantor's minimum liquidity, net worth, debt-to-worth ratios, etc.
- maximum distributions, or restrictions on distributions to partners or owners, before loan repayment.

Under certain circumstances, a service corporation of a federal savings association is permitted to hold real estate for investment and engage in real estate development subject to the limitations of 12 CFR 159.5. National banks generally are not permitted to engage in real estate development. A national bank is permitted, however, under 12 CFR 7.1006 to take a share in the profit or income generated from property as consideration for a loan although the borrower's obligation to repay principal may not be conditioned upon the receipt of profit or income. This is often referred to as a participating mortgage or equity kicker.

In determining whether an arrangement should be recorded as a loan, joint venture or a real estate loan investment, the guidance in Accounting Standards of Codification (ASC) Section 310-10-25 should be followed. Where the lender receives greater than 50 percent of the profits, the lender should account for the relationship as a real estate investment and the profits or losses recorded in accordance with ASC Topic 970. Where the lender receives 50 percent or less of the profits, the arrangement should be accounted for as a loan or joint venture, depending on the circumstances. An arrangement that contains risks and rewards that are similar to a loan (discussed in ASC Subsection 310-10-25-20) or where the arrangement is supported by a qualifying personal guarantee, it should be recorded as a loan and interest and fees should be recognized as income subject to recoverability; see ASC Topic 974. Otherwise, the arrangement should be accounted for as a joint venture consistent with ASC Subtopics 970-323 and 970-835. There are times when an ADC arrangement is initially appropriately classified as an investment or joint venture and should be reclassified to a loan. When the risk to the lender diminishes significantly, an evaluation should be completed to determine if it the arrangement should be reclassified to a loan under ASC Subsection 310-10-35-56.

Borrowing Base Lending

Tract development is often funded utilizing a borrowing base. The borrowing base is a revolving credit agreement that limits the bank's legally binding commitment to advance funds to the borrower. The borrowing base specifies the maximum amount the bank can lend to the borrower as a function of the collateral's type, value, eligibility criteria, and advance rates. The credit agreement also specifies a maximum commitment amount regardless of the amount of the borrowing base availability.

Typically, the borrowing base formula establishes different advance rates for each collateral type, such as land, developed lots, homes under construction and completed, and sold and unsold homes. The amount of collateral in each category and the corresponding advance rates limit the borrower's ability to draw additional funds. The advance rates are generally higher for collateral with lower development, construction, and marketing risk. For example, the advance rate for developed lots is likely to be lower than that for a completed home. In addition, advance rates may vary among borrowers. Generally, banks grant more liberal advance rates to borrowers that have greater financial strength. Collateral must meet specified eligibility criteria to be included in the borrowing base. These criteria commonly include limitations on the number of speculative units and the duration of time a completed unsold unit or finished vacant lot may remain in the borrowing base.

This type of facility enables the bank to control loan advances and proceeds from home sales. The funds available under the revolver are based on frequent (usually monthly) borrower-prepared reports, commonly referred to as a borrowing base certificate. The borrowing base certificate details and certifies the quantity and value of collateral in each category that meets the borrowing-base eligibility criteria and the total amount of the borrowing base (the outstanding balance of the facility plus any available funds). The bank should periodically perform on-site verification of the information provided by the borrower.

When developing the borrowing base formula, the bank should require the borrower to maintain appropriate levels of hard equity throughout the project's construction and marketing periods.

Interest Reserves

Banks should develop and implement a policy for using interest reserves in a manner that is consistent with safe and sound banking practices. Interest expense is an important element of a project budget and, like other construction costs, should be properly estimated with funds identified for its payment. An appropriate interest reserve ensures that sufficient funds are available to pay interest through the project's anticipated completion and lease-up, sale, or occupancy. Inappropriately administered reserves, however, can mask a poorly performing project, increase the bank's loss exposure, and have been a major contributor to banks' losses in ADC lending. For these reasons, interest reserves should be closely scrutinized by examiners.

When establishing the appropriate amount of interest reserves, the bank should evaluate the reasonableness of the development assumptions including potential changes in interest rates, the timing of expected disbursements and pay downs, and the time required for the completion and sale or lease-up of the project. If interest will not be funded by the bank, the bank should ensure there is sufficient equity to permit the bank to fund the interest if necessary while keeping the loan within appropriate loan-to-cost and LTV ratios, even if the borrower intends to pay interest from his or her own funds.

The use of interest reserves to fund interest payments for loans that should be amortizing such as stabilized properties or speculative purchases of raw land is not appropriate.

Banks are expected to maintain effective controls to monitor the status of the project and protect the adequacy of the interest reserve. During the lease-up period, any income from the project should ordinarily be applied to interest before interest reserves are applied. Once the cash flow is sufficient to cover the interest, no further draws on the reserve should be permitted to prevent the diversion of income that should be used to support the project.

The budgeted interest reserve is sometimes exhausted before the project is completed and lease-up or sale is achieved. This often occurs as a result of construction delays or a change in market conditions. In such cases, the borrower or guarantor should provide additional cash to cover interest payments or replenish the reserves. At times, should the borrower or guarantor be unable or unwilling to do this, banks have elected to increase or "repack" the interest reserve to keep the loan current, thereby potentially masking a nonperforming loan. The decision to revise the budget and repack the interest reserve with debt is a red flag signaling probable credit deterioration and should be clearly supported by the project's viability and the repayment capacity of the borrower in order to avoid criticism by examiners. This would include obtaining a new appraisal or evaluation and re-evaluating the feasibility of the project in the current market. If projections show that the timing and amount of projected cash flows will fully amortize the debt and support subsequent interest payments after the additional interest reserves are depleted, then the additional reserves and continued interest accrual may be appropriate.

While interest can be capitalized under the terms of a loan agreement, for reporting purposes, it is only appropriate when the borrower has the ability to repay the debt in the normal course of business.

ADC Loan Administration

The bank's loan administration function should have effective control procedures in place to ensure sound loan advances and that liens are paid and released. Effective controls should include segregation of duties, site inspections, budget monitoring, and dual approval of loan disbursements. Records should be maintained that demonstrate whether remaining funds are adequate to complete the project. The records should be complete and subject to independent audit.

Monitoring Progress of Construction Projects

Banks must monitor the progress of the projects they finance to ensure that the borrower's request for funds is appropriate for the particular stage of development with adequate funds remaining for completion. The bank must obtain accurate and timely inspection reports reflecting the status of the project so it may be alerted when the project is not proceeding as represented or planned.

To detect signs of financial problems in a project or with the developer, the bank should periodically review the developer's financial statements. This review should assess the liquidity, debt capacity, and cash flow of the developer. The review can help detect problems not only with the bank's own loan, but also potential problems arising from one of the developer's other projects that could act as a drain on the developer's resources. The bank also should review the borrower's major sources of cash and ascertain whether the source is dependent on the ongoing sale of real estate or infusions of capital.

An updated credit report can be used to determine whether there are any unpaid bills, whether vendors are being paid late, or whether suits or judgments have been entered against the borrower. In many localities, banks may also access weekly legal reports and trade reports to monitor the borrower's standing. The bank should also verify property tax payments to ensure that the developer has sufficient resources to make them and that delinquent taxes do not create a lien on the collateral.

Most construction budgets include amounts allocated for contingencies. These amounts are intended to cover reasonable but unexpected increases in construction costs, such as price increases in materials or the need to pay overtime because of delays in the shipment of materials or adverse weather. Cost overruns on a project may also be the result of poor projections or poor management. In these cases, the increased cost should ordinarily be covered by the borrower rather than by a draw-down on the loan amount budgeted for contingencies.

The bank should also guard against funds being misused to pay for extra costs not stipulated in the loan agreement. Examples of extra costs include rebuilding to meet specification changes not previously disclosed, starting a new project, paying subcontractors for work performed elsewhere, or paying for the developer's general overhead. The lender should be aware of the practice of front loading, whereby a builder deliberately overstates the cost of the work to be completed in the early stages of construction. If the bank does not detect this problem in the early stages of construction, there will almost certainly be insufficient loan funds to complete construction if there is a default.

Monitoring Commercial Construction Projects

An established loan administration process that continually monitors each project's progress, costs, and loan disbursements is essential to effectively controlling commercial construction risk. Banks should periodically schedule physical inspections of the project and evaluate the work performed against project design and budget. Banks often retain an independent construction consulting firm if they do not have the necessary in-house engineering, architectural, and construction expertise to perform this function.

Banks should obtain monthly reports of work completed, cost-to-date, cost-to-complete, construction deadlines, and loan funds remaining. Any changes in construction plans should be reviewed by competent staff or a construction consulting firm and approved and documented by the bank and take-out lender, if any. A significant number of change orders could indicate poor planning or project design, or problems in construction, and should be tracked and reflected in the project's budget.

Monthly leasing reports with rent rolls should be obtained from the borrower during the lease-up period, where applicable. The reports should be analyzed to monitor the progress of lease-up and to compare actual lease rates and other key terms with the underwriting pro forma and assumptions utilized in the appraisal. Material deviations from the plan can have an adverse effect on the value of the collateral and debt-service coverage. This may result in a higher-than-expected LTV upon completion and can endanger timely repayment. Extended lease-up periods can deplete the interest reserve prematurely and render the construction budget inadequate, requiring a contribution of additional equity or an unplanned increase in the loan amount.

The bank must monitor economic factors that could affect the project's success upon completion. Because the development, construction, and lease-up of a commercial project can span several years, the bank must continually assess the project's marketability and whether demand will continue to exist when the project is completed.

Monitoring Residential Tract Development Projects

In addition to periodically inspecting each house or unit during the course of construction, the bank should ensure that it obtains periodic reports reflecting progress on the entire project as compared against budgeted projections. These progress reports should be provided by the borrower on a monthly basis and should identify each lot or unit by number along with the style of house it may be improved with and its state of completion, the release and offering prices, and loan balance. The report should include the selling price, dates of sale for sold units, and the date of contract or closing.

Existing inventory, construction starts, and sales must be monitored to avoid excessive inventory buildup. The rate of absorption can be influenced by the housing product type; custom homes or homes on larger lots often tend to sell at a slower pace than homes built in tract developments.

The bank should establish criteria necessary to consider a unit "sold." OCC Bulletin 2010-42, "Sound Practices for Appraisals and Evaluations: Interagency Appraisal and Evaluation Guidelines" states that a unit may be considered presold if a buyer has entered into a binding contract to purchase the unit and has made a substantial and nonrefundable earnest money deposit. Further, the institution should obtain sufficient documentation that the buyer has entered into a legally binding sales contract and has obtained a written prequalification or commitment for permanent financing.

Lower than projected selling prices, slow sales, or excessive inventories relative to sales indicate that the borrower may have difficulty repaying the loan. Other problems, such as higher than expected costs or delays in completing construction, can also weaken the borrower's ability to repay.

On an ongoing basis, the bank should also monitor general economic conditions and other economic factors that could affect the marketing and selling of residential properties in the bank's lending areas. These factors could include housing prices, housing inventory, mortgage interest rates, consumer confidence, unemployment rate and job creation, existing and new home sales, household formation, and residential rental rates.

Disbursement of Construction Loans

Banks are expected to maintain effective policies and procedures governing the loan disbursement process. It is important that the bank's minimum borrower equity requirements are maintained throughout the development and construction periods and that sufficient funds are available to complete construction. Controls should include inspection processes, documentation of construction progress, preleasing activity and tracking presold units, and exception monitoring and reporting. The bank should not advance funds unless the funds are to be used solely for the project being financed and as stipulated in the draw request and governed by the loan agreement. The lender's title policy should be updated with each draw.

Banks generally disburse construction loan funds according to a standard payment plan or a progress payment plan. Either plan should be structured so that the amount of each construction draw is commensurate with improvements made as of the date of the inspection or certification provided by the bank.

Occasionally, rather than pay on a standard or progress payment plan, banks may disburse funds on a voucher basis whereby each bill or receipt is presented and either paid or reimbursed by the lender. This can increase the lender's administrative control but can also increase the lender's administrative burden.

Standard Payment Plan

A standard payment plan is normally used for residential and smaller commercial construction loans. Because residential construction projects usually consist of houses in various stages of construction, this plan establishes a predetermined schedule for fixed payments at the end of each specified stage of construction.

A standard payment plan for residential construction most commonly consists of five equal installments. The first four disbursements are made when construction has reached agreed-upon stages, verified by actual inspection of the property. As each house is completed and sold and the predetermined release price is paid to the bank, the bank releases its lien on that particular house. Except for some workout situations, excess net sales proceeds are remitted to the borrower. The final payment is made only after the legally stipulated period for mechanics' liens has expired.

Progress Payment Plan

The progress payment plan is normally used for commercial projects. Under a progress payment plan, the bank releases funds as the borrower completes certain phases of construction. The bank normally retains, or holds back, 10 percent to 20 percent of each payment to cover project cost overruns or outstanding bills from suppliers or subcontractors.

Under a progress payment plan, the borrower requests payment from the bank in the form of a construction draw request or certification of payment, which sets forth the funding request by construction phase and cost category. The borrower also certifies that the conditions of the loan agreement have been met, e.g., that all requested funds are being used for the project and that suppliers and subcontractors have been paid. The construction draw request should include waivers from the project's subcontractors and suppliers indicating that payment has been received for the work completed. After reviewing the draw request and independently confirming the progress of work, the bank then disburses funds for construction costs incurred, less the holdback.

The final draw on a commercial construction loan usually includes payment of the holdback as stipulated in the loan agreement. The draw is used by the borrower to pay all remaining expenses. Before releasing the final draw and disbursing the holdback, the bank should confirm that the borrower has obtained all waivers of liens or releases from the project's contractors, subcontractors, and suppliers. The bank also should obtain and review the final inspection report to confirm that the project is complete and meets building specifications. The bank also should confirm that the builder has obtained a certificate of occupancy from the governing building authority.

Income-Producing Real Estate Lending

This section of the booklet discusses term financing for stabilized, income-producing properties. Term financing may refinance construction or bridge loans on properties that have reached stabilization, refinance other term financing, or finance the acquisition of stabilized properties. Term loans that refinance construction loans are sometimes referred to as permanent loans or take-outs.

Term loans are also provided by other types of lenders including life insurance companies, pension funds, and commercial mortgage-backed securities (also referred to as CMBS or conduits). Life insurance companies and pension funds often have long-term investment needs and find terms of 10 years or longer on a fixed-rate basis attractive. CMBS investors like the ability to buy tranches of a CMBS pool that match their preferred term, risk appetite, and yield needs. Loans from these sources usually feature loan terms of 10 years or more with fixed rates and are commonly nonrecourse.

Underwriting Income-Producing Real Estate Loans

Banks are expected to establish clear underwriting standards consistent with the type of income-producing CRE lending performed. This section of the booklet discusses key underwriting considerations for income-producing real estate loans. Refer to the "Underwriting Standards" section of this booklet and the "Interagency Guidelines for Real Estate Lending Policies," 12 CFR 34, subpart D, appendix A (national banks) and appendix to 12 CFR 160.101 (federal savings associations).

Market Analysis

The performance of income-producing real estate is significantly influenced by local and regional economic conditions. Banks are expected to monitor conditions in the bank's lending area as part of a sound credit risk management function. Periodic market analysis should be performed for the various property types and geographic markets represented in the bank's portfolio. Sales prices, rental rates and lease terms, vacancy rates, available inventory, absorption rates, construction starts, and permits granted are examples of useful market data. The level of detail and complexity of the analysis should correspond to the level of risk inherent in the bank's lending activities.

Income-Generating Capacity of Real Estate

Because repayment of loans that finance income-producing real estate is typically primarily dependent on the property's ability to service debt from cash flow and collateral value is largely determined by a property's NOI, it is important to carefully analyze and fully understand the income generating capacity of the real estate.

A property's cash flow and NOI projections should be carefully reviewed to ensure they are reasonable and supported. Any information included in the analysis that seems questionable or is inadequately supported should be challenged. The review should consider

- historical, current and projected rental rates, operating expenses, capital expenditures, vacancy and absorption rates.
- lease renewal trends and anticipated rents.
- volume and trends in past due leases.
- comparable rental rates, operating expenses, and sales prices.
- terms of current leases.
- direct capitalization rates and, if appropriate, discount rates.

Banks should consider each of the factors under normal and stressed conditions. For example, as real estate income and prices rise in periods of economic growth, lenders should stress test capitalization rates and DSCRs to determine whether a property will remain viable during a period of economic stress.

Unlike cash-flow analysis, the NOI analysis may assume market rates of vacancy that are above or below actual vacancy rates and expenses that may not represent an actual or immediate cash expense, such as management fees for owner-occupied properties and reserves for capital replacements. When loan documents contain debt-service coverage covenants, the definitions of income and expenses should be clearly defined.

While tax returns can be helpful in analyzing property income and expenses, some outlays for capital items may be shown as an expense on the tax return but excluded as an expense for determining NOI. Capital items, for purposes of calculating NOI, are typically reflected in the replacement reserve. Also, tax returns may represent income and expenses on a cash basis only, showing only the income and expenses that were actually received or paid during the year. For example, a tax return for a property for which real estate taxes were not paid during that year would understate expenses and overstate income. This can also be the case with operating statements that are prepared on a cash basis. For this reason, it is helpful to compare reported expenses with expenses incurred by comparable properties, adjusted for supported variances and lease terms. An important objective of the underwriting process is to develop an NOI that represents a stabilized estimate of income and expenses.

In addition to assessing property cash flows, the bank should also analyze the ability and willingness of the borrower or guarantor(s) to provide support when needed. This is discussed in the "Analysis of Borrower's and Guarantor's Financial Condition" section of this booklet.

Value Analysis

The income approach to value converts expected future NOI into present value through direct capitalization or discounted cash-flow analysis. Direct capitalization estimates the value of a property by capitalizing the NOI using an appropriate capitalization rate (commonly referred to as the "cap" rate). This is accomplished by dividing the NOI by the capitalization rate. This method is appropriate when applied to stabilized NOI and the future income stream is expected to be stable. The discounted cash-flow method discounts expected future NOI to be received over a specified holding period and the expected net sales price at the end of that period by an appropriate discount rate to determine the net present value of a property. This method is useful in estimating the as-is value of properties that have not reached stabilized occupancy or values of properties that are expected to experience material fluctuations in income.

The discount and cap rates used in estimating property income and values should reflect reasonable expectations for the rate of return that investors and lenders require under normal, orderly and sustainable market conditions.

Other factors that should be considered include age, condition, location, and how the property compares with competitive properties, including a comparison of rental rates, expenses, and sales prices. Collateral considerations for various property types are discussed in the "Underwriting Considerations by Property Type" section of this booklet.

The financing of unique or specialized types of property presents additional risk and more difficult valuation issues. This type of lending should be specifically addressed in a bank's underwriting and valuation policies. These types of property are normally less marketable and more difficult to liquidate should the borrower default, particularly if a bank is forced to sell the property during periods of real estate market weakness. Marketing and holding costs and the cost to convert the property to alternative uses with greater market demand are some of the valuation issues presented by these properties.

Loan Structure

Banks engaged in income-producing property lending are expected to extend prudently underwritten and structured loans consistent with the risk profile of the property and the risk appetite of the bank. Loan policies should establish prudent standards for loan structure such as tenor, amortization, guarantees, equity, and covenants that are within the risk parameters approved by the board of directors and consistent with supervisory guidance and regulations. All loans have risk; prudent lending requires the bank to identify risks, assess their nature and magnitude, and structure the loan in a way that sufficiently mitigates them.

Tenor

Proper tenor selection can help mitigate risks that are associated with future events. While banks may view longer terms as helping to win business and retain assets longer, they also bring higher risks. When real estate markets deteriorate and property performance declines, a longer term may prevent the bank from requiring the borrower to contribute additional equity or otherwise restructuring the loan in a way that considers a property's performance. Loan covenants that establish standards for property performance can serve to mitigate this risk.

Amortization

The timing of repayment, as determined by the amortization period and method or principal curtailments, is a critical consideration in prudent loan structuring. Interest-only periods should be limited to construction or stabilization periods. Renewals, refinancing, or extensions of loans on an interest-only basis may indicate troubled loans.

Although longer amortization periods can decrease the likelihood of payment default by allowing for higher debt-service coverage, they can increase the loss, given default and the balloon risk at maturity when the loan does not fully amortize over the term. The amortization period should consider the risks to cash flow during the term and the anticipated collateral value at maturity.

While OCC guidance does not dictate maximum tenors, prudent lenders generally consider 30 years to be a reasonable maximum for real estate. While a property may have a longer useful life, a matching amortization period may result in such nominal principal reduction during the initial years that maintaining adequate collateral coverage throughout the loan term becomes uncertain.

For income-producing properties, a range of 15 to 30 years would be appropriate in most cases, with stabilized multifamily dwellings at the higher end (up to 30 years), hotels at the lower end (generally not more than 20 years), and office, retail, and industrial properties in the middle (generally 25 years). This is consistent with the historical predictability of both the cash flows and the depreciated values for each property type. Other factors to consider include the property's class (A, B, or C), stability and financial strength of the tenant base, and rent rates compared with the market, as well as economic and demographic trends, such as unemployment, local market supply, and population growth. The "Office" section of this booklet includes a discussion of property class.

The amortization for restructured CRE loans should also be reasonable and reflect the underlying project risk. For a single-family residential development loan where the project is slow but sales continue, and the guarantor has the ability and willingness to supplement payment through re-margining of the credit, an amortization period of up to 10 years may be appropriate. Conversely, for a project that has completely stalled and has no guarantor that can reliably supplement principal payments, such an amortization schedule would not be appropriate. The workout plan for such a loan should include repayment terms more similar to those for the purchase of raw land.

For condominium and single-family residential projects that convert to rentals and tend to depreciate at an accelerated rate relative to owned units, amortization periods of less than 30 years generally would be reasonable. Much of the determination of what is reasonable depends on an evaluation of the individual project. Some banks restructure these types of loans as mortgage loans in the developer's name. Banks making such loans should have well-defined, board-approved policies for rental properties, and these developer loans should fit into those underwriting parameters.

Some types of income-producing property loans have a built-in restructuring trigger; such is the case with a five-year tenor in which payments are based on a 20-year amortization. In these situations, the bank is able to periodically review the strength of the primary and secondary repayment sources and re-underwrite the credit. A common question from examiners in these situations is whether, at the end of the first five-year period (or at any renewal date), it would be inappropriate for the bank to re-amortize the remaining balance over 20 years. The answer depends on the specific transaction. If the sources of repayment and other structural components are, in combination, adequate to protect the lender over the next 20 years, then re-amortizing the remaining balance may be supportable. Bankers and examiners, however, should note that re-amortizing the remaining balance over the original period reduces the payment amount, which in effect diverts cash flow from the bank to the borrower. The rationale for accepting diversion of that cash flow should be clearly addressed in the bank's credit approval document.

LTV Ratio

The determination of an appropriate LTV should consider the same criteria as those for amortization. Loans secured by properties having less volatility in cash flow and value may merit higher LTVs while loans secured by higher-risk properties should mitigate this higher risk with more equity. SLTVs are important for reporting, supervisory, and risk management purposes; however, they do not establish a safe harbor. The determination of an appropriate LTV should consider the particular risks presented by each loan. The bank's lending policy should establish prudent criteria for acceptable LTVs that consider the risks posed by various loan and property types.

Debt-Service Coverage Ratio

The DSCR, calculated by dividing the NOI by the annual debt service, measures the ability of the property to service its debt. The determination of an appropriate DSCR should consider the loan amortization period and the expected volatility of the cash flow. In some cases, a lower DSCR may be a prudent trade-off for a shorter amortization period or appropriate for properties with stable and certain cash flows, such as those with long-term net leases to highly creditworthy tenants. Properties that have volatile cash flows, such as hotels or owner occupants with uneven earnings, may warrant a higher ratio.

Debt Yield

Debt yield is the ratio of NOI to debt. It is calculated by dividing the NOI by the loan amount (typically senior debt only) with the quotient expressed as a percent. Debt yield provides a measurement of risk that is independent of the interest rate, amortization period, and capitalization rate. Lower debt yields indicate higher leverage. This measure can be especially useful during periods of low interest and capitalization rates where loan amounts established by using the DSCR and LTV ratio may be prudent only as long as the low rate environment is sustained. Debt yields that reflect normalized or higher-rate levels can be used to establish stressed loan amounts that are less vulnerable to higher-rate environments. Debt yield also permits banks or examiners to utilize a common metric to quickly size a loan or assess its relative risk. While appropriate debt yields vary according to market conditions and property types, 10 percent is generally considered a minimum acceptable yield with higher yields recommended for riskier properties. Debt yield, when used, must be considered along with other criteria and loan amounts must always be supported by prudent DSCR and LTV ratios.

Underwriting Considerations by Property Type

Examiners should understand the unique characteristics and risks associated with various types of properties, and banks should establish prudent policies that consider these characteristics and risks for each loan type they finance. General considerations for the primary property types are discussed in this section. Underwriting metrics are provided only for general guidance and varies by market, property type, and building characteristics. Appraisals of similar properties and third-party surveys can provide information that is more specific to a property's characteristics and market.

Office

Office buildings can be classified as suburban or central business district (CBD) properties and graded in terms of quality from A to C. Class A properties are newer, recently rehabilitated, or very well-maintained properties built of high-quality materials offering retail and other amenities. Class B properties are older or of average construction with few or no amenities and average desirability, while Class C offers space that may be outdated or plain but functional.

Important characteristics to consider when evaluating an office property are the aesthetics of the design and quality of materials, availability of parking, access to public transportation or major roads, and proximity to hotels, shopping, and other amenities. Also important are the size and configurability of the floors (the floor plate) to accommodate tenants requiring various amounts of space, adequacy of elevator service, and the ability to meet current and future technology requirements.

Medical office buildings have unique requirements, including additional plumbing and wiring to accommodate examination room fixtures and equipment. Consequently, costs for construction and tenant improvements are higher than conventional office buildings. These buildings are often located near other medical service providers, such as hospitals, and may feature pharmacies and lab facilities.

Office buildings are usually leased on a gross basis (expenses paid by the landlord) with the tenant typically responsible for expenses directly related to occupancy such as utilities and janitorial. Because terms can vary from lease to lease, however, lease agreements should always be reviewed to determine which expenses are the landlord's responsibility. Lease terms are typically for periods of three, five, or seven years.

Replacement reserves for office properties are underwritten on an annual, per-square-foot basis and varies depending on the property's age and condition. Management fees are typically underwritten from 3 percent to 5 percent of effective gross income, depending on the number of tenants.

Costs to re-lease space are important underwriting considerations. These costs include leasing commissions and the cost of tenant improvements for new and renewing tenants. Leasing commissions are calculated as a percentage of total lease payments with typical underwriting assumptions of 4 percent for new leases and 2 percent for renewals. Expenses for tenant improvements are higher for new tenants than for renewing tenants and can vary widely depending on the market and building class. The re-leasing costs can be projected by an analysis of the rent roll and utilizing an assumption about the probability of renewals with 60 percent to 65 percent being typical. Re-leasing costs are not always considered as an operating expense in calculating NOI but are an important consideration when analyzing cash flow.

Retail

There are many types of retail properties. They may be anchored, with major tenants that generate traffic for other tenants and provide financial stability, or unanchored. They range in size from very small neighborhood centers serving their immediate communities to super regional malls that may have 1 million square feet or more drawing from very large trade areas.

Demographics, including population concentration and income levels, along with vehicular traffic volume, site configuration, ease of ingress and egress, parking, surrounding residential density, and tenant mix are all important in determining the success of retail properties.

Appropriate site characteristics are critical to the success of retail properties. Some things to consider include the following.

- The traffic count should be suitable for the retail type; small neighborhood centers can be successful on tertiary or secondary roads while larger properties, such as power centers or major malls, require location on or access to primary arteries.
- Properties and signage should be readily visible to passing traffic; sites that are parallel to the primary source of traffic flow are generally superior to sites that are perpendicular to the road, having less frontage and visibility.
- Traffic control devices and turning lanes should permit easy access for vehicles passing in either direction at all times of the day.

Lease terms generally vary by retail type and tenant. Considerations include the following.

- Lease terms typically range from five to 10 years with anchor tenants often signing leases of 20 to 25 years with options to renew.
- Leases are commonly written on a net basis with tenants reimbursing the landlord for common area maintenance (CAM), including landscaping, refuse collection, taxes, insurance, and lighting of parking lots and walkways, with the landlord usually responsible for the roof and outer walls. Because terms can vary from lease to lease, however, lease agreements should always be reviewed to determine which expenses are the landlord's responsibility.
- Anchor tenants may pay a flat rate plus a percentage of their annual sales (percentage rent). Percentage rents may vary considerably and are inherently less predictable. The flat rate should be high enough to dissuade the tenant from ceasing operations while maintaining possession in order to prevent the landlord from leasing to a competitor. It

is desirable for an anchor tenant's lease to require continued operations so that the tenant may be replaced if it ceases to operate.

- Some lease clauses may call for a decrease in rents or permit termination if an anchor tenant ceases operations (co-tenancy clauses). These clauses make the success of anchor tenants even more critical to the viability of the property.

Tenant improvements provided for retail tenants tend to be minimal, with the landlord usually delivering a so-called "white box" (primed drywall and a concrete floor) to the tenant who is responsible for finishing the space.

Replacement reserves for retail properties are underwritten on an annual per-square-foot basis and varies depending on the property's age and condition. Management fees are typically underwritten at 3 percent to 5 percent of effective gross income, exclusive of reimbursements.

Re-leasing costs consist mostly of leasing commissions, which are usually underwritten at 4 percent of the total lease payments for new tenants and 2 percent for renewing tenants as determined by the underwriting assumptions with respect to tenant renewal.

Industrial

Industrial properties include manufacturing, light industrial, warehouse, and distribution facilities. While industrial properties can be located in older or redeveloped urban areas or in the suburbs, their proximity to transportation is an important factor. This is also true of distribution facilities where access to major highways is of crucial importance.

Industrial buildings can vary widely in size, typically ranging from several thousand to several hundred thousand square feet and may be single- or multi-tenant. Office space usually comprises about 10 to 20 percent of the total square footage of these properties.

Physical characteristics that can accommodate the operations of prospective tenants are critical considerations. Industrial properties usually feature ceiling heights that range from 18 to 30 feet and require sufficient truck bays with a site large enough to permit the maneuvering of large trucks. Electrical capacity and floor thickness are important considerations. Properties that do not meet these criteria may be at a significant disadvantage relative to competing properties.

Industrial properties having a higher percentage of office space, sometimes 50 percent or more, are commonly referred to as flex, research and development, or high-tech. The industrial portions of these buildings tend to have office-like ceiling heights with few or no truck bays. These properties share many characteristics with office properties, and these characteristics should be considered when the properties are underwritten.

Industrial properties as a group pose the highest risk of environmental contamination and merit close review of past and intended uses and investigation of their current environmental condition.

Manufacturing facilities are often built to accommodate a specific user's needs. The adaptability of the building to meet the needs of other potential users is an important underwriting consideration.

Leases for single-tenant industrial properties are usually written on a net basis with the landlord responsible for maintenance of the roof and outer walls only. Because terms can vary from lease to lease, however, lease agreements should always be reviewed to determine which expenses are the landlord's responsibility.

Landlords for multi-tenant properties would typically be responsible for CAM and require reimbursement for this from the tenant. Lease terms of three to five years are common. Replacement reserves for industrial properties are underwritten on an annual per-square-foot basis and vary depending on the age and condition of the property. Management fees typically range from 3 percent to 4 percent, depending on the number of tenants.

Multifamily

Multifamily rental properties fill an important need in many communities; they can be more affordable than owner-occupied housing and offer relatively short-term housing solutions. Multifamily, or apartment, properties have historically been one of the most stable property types, despite typical leases of one year and higher rates of tenant turnover than other property types.

Management ability is critical to the success of these properties; inept or inexperienced management is a major cause of difficulty for loans financing multifamily dwellings. Mitigating tenant turnover requires a constant marketing effort and management must retain tenants when possible by being attentive to their needs. In addition to attracting and retaining tenants, management must do an effective job of collecting rents. Even though a review of the rent roll might indicate a high rate of occupancy, actual collections should be examined to determine the true economic occupancy and evaluate the competency of management and the effectiveness of its collection efforts. Whether properties are self-managed or managed by a third party, the manager's ability and experience should be carefully evaluated.

Important general considerations for multifamily properties include

- **demographics:** income levels, age distribution, rate of household formations, and household sizes.
- **economic factors:** affordability of entry-level single-family housing versus renting, strength of local economy, local employment conditions including current levels and trends, trends in the value of single-family housing, current levels and trends for local rents, and vacancy.
- **location factors:** local quality of life; proximity to shopping, recreation, and employment; school system; and availability of land for future residential development.
- **local and state laws:** rent control and or stabilization programs, co-op/condominium conversion rules, low income housing programs.

Property-specific considerations include

- occupancy history.
- collection losses.
- rents as compared with competitive properties.
- management quality.
- ingress and egress.
- quality of construction, age, and condition of improvements.
- parking availability and convenience.
- amenities as compared with competitive properties.
- availability of individual unit metering for utilities.

Lack of proper maintenance can pose a significant risk to the viability of multifamily properties. Undercapitalized borrowers may neglect needed maintenance when cash flows are inadequate which can result in increased turnover and vacancies. Deferred maintenance can significantly affect loan losses and expenses in the event of foreclosure. An inspection of the property should determine how many of the vacant units are rentable in their current condition; cash-strapped borrowers sometimes "cannibalize" vacant units of appliances, heating units, and other items when replacements are needed. It is important that banks monitor property maintenance and improvements to ensure they are timely and appropriate. Banks should ensure that cash flow is adequate to provide for necessary replacements and upgrades over time.

Historical operating expenses should be carefully analyzed. Operating expenses would usually be expected to range from 35 percent to 45 percent of revenue. Older properties, those with more amenities, and properties where the landlord provides heat, water, or electricity as part of the rent (usually because of lack of separate metering) represent the upper end of the range.

A multifamily property is typically underwritten with management fees of 5 percent of revenues. Replacement reserves for multifamily properties are underwritten on an annual per-unit basis and vary based on the age and condition of the property.

Hospitality

The hospitality industry is highly sensitive to trends in leisure and business spending. Hospitality properties have historically experienced considerable volatility in income and value. Hotel operations can be complex and may have a sizable non-real estate component. Successful hotel lending requires specialized knowledge and should not be undertaken without an adequate understanding of the hospitality business.

Hotels may be full or limited service. Full service hotels offer a number of amenities including dining and room service, convenience retail, higher service-staff levels, banquet and convention facilities, recreational facilities, and business support services. Consequently, full service hotels derive a significant portion of their income from non-room-related activities. Non-room revenue and expense centers include banquet, food and beverage, and others.

Limited service hotels and motels offer no or limited food service and limited meeting space. Location in close proximity to restaurants is an important consideration for limited service hotels.

A hotel's franchise, or "flag," can be an important factor in the success of a hotel. Flagged hotels benefit from a central reservation service and guest loyalty programs. Other franchise benefits include brand identity, operating guidance, strategic support, uniform standards, training, and marketing and sales support.

In addition to economic conditions, the following property-specific factors should be considered:

- Current and historical profitability and trends.
- Management quality.
- Reputation of the franchisor.
- Franchise agreement including duration and termination rights.
- Property age, condition, and amenities.
- Age, condition, and quality of furniture, fixtures, and equipment (FF&E) and replacement needs.
- Revenue seasonality.
- Proximity to transportation and demand generators such as office and recreational facilities.
- Adequacy and convenience of parking.

Common performance metrics for hotels are occupancy and average daily rate (ADR) and revenue per available room (RevPAR). The ADR is calculated by dividing the room revenue by the number of rooms occupied for a given period. This calculation should exclude complimentary rooms or other occupancy that do not generate revenue. RevPAR is calculated by multiplying a hotel's ADR by its occupancy rate.

Other income and expenses, such as for food and beverage, banquet, telephone, or Internet use, are segregated into separate departments. Expenses that are not directly attributable to a department, such as management, franchise, sales and marketing fees, and repairs and maintenance, are recorded as unallocated expenses. Real estate taxes and insurance are allocated to fixed expenses.

Studies of industry performance metrics provide an important comparative reference in underwriting hotels. These studies are commercially available and should be utilized in the bank's underwriting process. While an analysis of historical income and expenses should include a comparison with industry benchmarks to test for reasonableness, the following underwriting considerations provide guidance in analyzing a hotel's income and expenses.

- **Franchise fees:** Usually underwritten at the higher of actual or 4 to 6 percent of total revenues.
- **Management fees:** Typically expected to be 4 to 5 percent of gross revenues.
- **Fixed expenses:** Expenses for property taxes, real and personal, should reflect the actual property tax assessment. Insurance should reflect the actual expense and include premiums for insuring the real and personal property.
- **Replacement reserves:** Reserves for FF&E typically range from 4 to 6 percent of total revenues.
- **Profit margins:** Vary according to type, franchise, and location. Margins for full service properties typically range from 20 to 30 percent while limited service properties generally range from 30 to 40 percent. Luxury resorts typically range from 20 to 25 percent with extended-stay suites usually ranging from 35 to 42 percent.

Appraisals of hotel properties, in addition to the market value of the real estate, may also include values of personal property, such as FF&E, and intangibles, such as goodwill. The sum of these values is sometimes referred to as the "going-concern value." The value, however, of non-real property, such as personal property and intangibles, cannot be used to support federally related transactions; value opinions, such as "going-concern value," "value in use," or a special value to a specific property user may not be used as market value for federally related transactions. An appraisal report that elicits a value of the enterprise, such as "going-concern value," must allocate that value among the components of the total value. Traditionally, the three components are described as: (1) market value of the real estate, (2) personal property value, and (3) value of intangibles. The bank may rely only on the real estate's market value in these appraisals to support the federally related transaction. A separate loan may be used to finance the personal property or intangibles. For further information, see OCC Bulletin 2010-42, "Sound Practices for Appraisals and Evaluations: Interagency Appraisal and Evaluation Guidelines."

Residential Health Care

Residential health care facilities typically include independent living, assisted living, and nursing homes. The most significant distinction among these is the level of care provided. While facilities are most often dedicated to one level of care, some may provide a continuum of services.

Independent living, sometimes referred to as congregate care, provides the lowest level of care. The residents do not require daily assistance with living activities and enjoy a high degree of mobility. The facilities share many of the features and amenities of multifamily properties with such additional features as dining rooms and communal living areas. The facilities may offer meals, laundry, and housekeeping. No health care is provided. These properties are not regulated and do not qualify for government reimbursement. Income is generated mostly from unit rental.

Assisted-living facilities provide a range of services for the elderly and disabled that can include meals, laundry, housekeeping, transportation, and assistance with daily living activities, such as dressing and bathing. Assisted-living facilities may be subject to state regulation with varying levels of health care permitted. When more acute medical care is permitted and provided, government reimbursement may be available.

Nursing homes provide 24-hour non-acute medical care and provide the highest level of living assistance and medical care. Nursing homes are highly regulated and, like hospitals, are subject to state certificates of need. Government reimbursement is a common source of payment.

The demand for residential health care facilities is strongly correlated with local demographics; residents want to live in locations convenient to their families, with older populations generating greater demand. The bank should consider the quality, reputation, and experience of management. Other considerations are adequacy of staffing, staff turnover, the condition and location of the facility, and the quality of care and services.

Assisted-living facilities and nursing homes are sensitive to government reimbursement programs; state and federal policies affecting qualification criteria and reimbursement rates are important considerations in the analysis of these properties. The mix of private and government pay can be a useful measurement in determining the sensitivity of these properties to changes in government reimbursement policies.

Religious Organization Facilities

Religious organizations are nonprofit, corporate entities that are either owned by the membership or by part of a denominational hierarchy. Loans to religious organizations are generally for the acquisition, construction, or expansion of facilities used in worship, community programs, schools, or other related activities.

Unlike many other real estate loans, reliance on collateral liquidation as a secondary source of repayment for these properties can be complicated by the highly specialized nature of the collateral and the reputation risk presented by foreclosure.

Underwriting a loan to a religious organization involves assessing the trend, level, and stability of income and expenses and determining the cash flow available for debt service. Primary income generally consists of tithes, offerings, other ongoing contributions or giving, and other sources of revenue, such as school or day-care income. Nonrecurring income, such as special one-time gifts and income from fund drives or capital campaigns, are regarded as secondary sources of income. The bank should assess a religious organization's primary income over at least a three-year period and closely examine any significant variances. Fixed expenses include general and administrative expenses, debt expenses and clergy and staff expenses.

Discretionary expenses can include ministry, outreach, and mission program-related expenses. A comprehensive financial analysis should consider the ratio of the loan amount to the gross annual receipts and the ratio of proposed annual debt service to gross annual receipts. Because facilities used for worship are not income-producing properties per se, valuation of these facilities relies heavily on the market and cost approaches.

In conducting its due diligence, the bank should consider the

- history of the organization and membership trends.
- history or prior experience with building programs.
- stability and experience of clergy, staff, and lay member leaders.
- hierarchical structure and governance in order to assess other obligors and assets available to support the loan.
- level of commitment from the members.

The collateral, loan terms, and interest rates on the loans necessarily vary depending on the nature of the religious organization and its activities. Banks should conduct ongoing monitoring of trends in revenues, expenses, and membership.

Monitoring Income-Producing Property

Loan covenants should require the submission of periodic financial information pertaining to the project, borrowing entities, and guarantors, if any. The frequency of the required property information should consider the stability of the property. For a property with few tenants and long-term leases that extend beyond the loan term or stabilized multifamily properties, annual operating statements and rent rolls may be adequate. Properties that are in lease-up or nonresidential properties that have many tenants or frequent lease expirations, however, could require the collection of monthly, quarterly, or semiannual information. The information that is collected should be analyzed in a timely manner to assess financial performance and compliance with any financial or performance covenants.

Banks should carefully manage the process for the collection and analysis of the information. Receipt and analysis should be tracked so that management can evaluate the effectiveness of its monitoring program. Ensuring that all borrowers and guarantors submit the information in a timely manner can be challenging and full compliance may be rarely achieved. Nevertheless, the bank should be able to demonstrate that, when borrowers or guarantors are unresponsive to information requests, its efforts to collect this information remain continuous and diligent.

Banks should monitor the timely payment of real estate taxes. Delinquent real estate taxes threaten the bank's interest in the collateral and are nearly always an indicator of a distressed property, borrower, or guarantor. There are many vendors that monitor the payment of real estate taxes. Most governmental units now make this information available online and this may enable a bank's own staff to monitor tax delinquencies directly.

Periodic property inspections should be performed to verify that the property is being adequately maintained and that tenants and vacancies have been accurately reported in the rent roll. Particular attention should be given to troubled properties and properties with troubled borrowers or guarantors.

Other Types of Income-Producing Real Estate Lending

Investor-Owned Residential Real Estate

Investor-owned residential real estate (IORR) is one- to four-family residential real estate where the primary repayment source is rental income and may be supported by the borrower's personal income.

Typically, IORR repayment sources have risk characteristics that are more similar to CRE than those of owner-occupied one- to four-family residential loans. Repayment sources for IORR loans may be volatile and highly leveraged in cases where the borrowers have multiple financed properties. Therefore, banks should have credit risk management policies and processes suitable for the risks specific to IORR lending. These policies and processes should cover loan underwriting standards, loan identification and portfolio monitoring expectations, allowance for loan and lease losses (ALLL) methodologies, and internal risk assessment and rating systems.

IORR lending should follow the standards for real estate lending as discussed in this booklet. It is important that the policy address an appropriate amortization period for IORR loans that considers both the property's useful life and the predictability of its future value. The policy should also consider the need for controls to monitor and mitigate risk. These could include the use of loan covenants, requirements for periodic financial analysis, and the need for a willing and financially capable guarantor. Further, IORR loan policies should establish underwriting standards pertaining to appropriate owner equity (LTV), acceptable appraisal or valuation methods, insurance requirements, and ongoing collateral monitoring.

Borrowers may finance multiple properties through one or more banks. Underwriting standards and the complexity of risk analysis should increase as the number of properties financed for a borrower and related parties increases. When a borrower finances multiple IORR properties, a comprehensive global cash-flow analysis of the borrower is generally necessary to properly underwrite and administer the credit relationship. In such cases, bank management should analyze and administer the relationship on a consolidated basis.

Identification of IORR properties is an important first step in measuring potential risk. Once identified, IORR properties should be segregated from other residential loans so that the bank can effectively manage the risk. The OCC recognizes that borrowers can convert homes into rentals without notifying their bank, and that banks may not have historically identified or structured loans to allow for the heightened monitoring that is generally required for IORR loans. Banks should make every effort to properly identify, monitor, and structure IORR loan relationships. Such efforts would include banks taking steps to strengthen their ability to monitor and control the credit relationship, where possible, on known IORR loans. Banks that have not previously distinguished between IORR loans and owner-occupied one- to four-family residential loans should implement methods to draw clear distinctions.

Banks should ensure that ALLL methodologies appropriately consider factors to reflect the risk of loss inherent in the IORR portfolio. Individually impaired IORR loans should be evaluated in accordance with ASC Subtopic 310-10 (formerly Financial Accounting Standards or FAS 114). Loans that are not individually impaired may be evaluated as an ASC Subtopic 450-20 (formerly FAS 5) pool. Until management information systems (MIS) are capable of IORR identification and segmentation, management should consider this unquantified risk when making qualitative adjustments to the ALLL analysis. Amounts incorporated into the ALLL methodology for IORR loans may be reflected within an ASC Subtopic 450-20 pool that is separate from owner-occupied one- to four-family residential loans.

The OCC expects banks to have credit risk management systems that produce accurate and timely risk ratings. Applying a rating system similar to that used for CRE lending is generally appropriate for an IORR portfolio. In some cases, however, the bank may have a separate rating system designed specifically for this type of lending. The risk assessment and rating process should not rely solely on delinquency status. The complexity of the ongoing analysis and risk rating should be commensurate with the number of properties financed globally by the borrower.

IORR loans are not specifically addressed within the scope of the interagency Uniform Retail Credit Classification and Account Management Policy (Retail Policy Statement). Banks have sometimes applied the classification time frames and the 180-day delinquency charge-off requirement for real estate loans from this policy to IORR loans. Using the classification time frames and the 180-day delinquency charge-off requirements is acceptable as an outer limit for IORR. Banks should, however, classify loans and recognize losses sooner if the circumstances on these loans meet the interagency classification definitions, which are consistent for both retail and commercial loans. Deviation from the minimum classification guidelines outlined in the interagency Retail Policy Statement is warranted if underwriting standards, risk management, or account management standards are weak and present unreasonable credit risk. For further guidance and CRE risk management expectations and classification, refer to OCC Bulletin 2009-32, "Commercial Real Estate (CRE) Loans: Guidance on Prudent CRE Loan Workouts," which conveys interagency guidance on the topic.

Banks should continue to report IORR loans that meet the call report[8] definition of one- to four-family residential lending in that category. IORR loans continue to qualify as residential real property loans under HOLA. IORR loans qualify for the 50 percent risk-based capital category if certain regulatory requirements are met. IORR loans that do not meet the criteria fall into a higher risk-based capital category. Refer to the call report instructions and the OCC's capital regulations for further detail on these topics.

Ground Leases

Banks may finance land that is to be leased to a tenant that constructs its own improvements or finance the tenant's improvements on ground that is leased from the ground owner.

---

[8] Consolidated Reports of Condition and Income, Federal Financial Institutions Examination Council (FFIEC)

Ground lease transactions involve various property interests and values: fee-simple, leased-fee, and leasehold interests. Fee-simple interest is the ownership as unencumbered by any other interest; leased-fee interest is an ownership interest held as a landlord (the lessor) with the rights of use and occupancy conveyed by a lease to a tenant; and the leasehold interest is the right held by a tenant (the lessee) for use and occupancy as conveyed by the landlord. Care should be taken in commissioning and reviewing the appraisal to ensure that the market value of the appropriate interest is obtained and used to support the loan.

At the end of the ground-lease term, the leasehold improvements revert to the lessor. For this reason, the value of a collateral leasehold interest diminishes over time and has no value upon maturity of the lease. In recognition of this, when the loan does not fully amortize before loan maturity, the expiration of the ground lease should extend sufficiently beyond the amortization period, customarily 20 years, to support refinancing and to ensure that adequate borrower equity in the project is retained. If the loan does fully amortize during the loan term, a lease term extending 10 years beyond the loan maturity is usually considered sufficient. In calculating debt-service coverage, the ground rent should be deducted as an expense.

The leasehold lender is in the most secure position when the land-owner subordinates his or her interest by granting the bank a first lien on the land to secure the bank's note financing the leasehold interest. If this is not possible, the bank should ensure that provisions of the lease agreement include a notice to the bank of tenant default under the ground lease and gives the lender the right, but not the obligation, to cure any defaults.

When the bank finances the ground lessor's leased-fee interest, the bank may lend up to the lesser of 65 percent of market value or cost of the land for its acquisition and then fund up to the appropriate SLTV of the market value of the borrower's leased-fee interest upon the completed construction of the lessee's improvements. In the case of a commercial property, for example, the SLTV limit would be 85 percent of the borrower's leased-fee interest upon completion of all construction.

When the bank finances the tenant's leasehold improvements, the maximum SLTV for construction would be up to a maximum of the relevant SLTV of the market value of the leasehold interest for construction (e.g., 80 percent of the value of the leasehold interest for a commercial property), and once construction is complete, the appropriate SLTV for the type of completed property. In the case of a commercial property, this would be 85 percent of the leasehold interest market value.

When the bank holds a junior lien, the sum of the debt and all senior liens should not exceed the relevant SLTV utilizing the fee-simple market value.

The SLTV limits represent the maximum permissible LTV that meets the supervisory guidelines. The LTV ratio is only one of several important credit factors to be considered when underwriting a real estate loan. Because of these other factors, the establishment of these supervisory limits should not be interpreted to mean that loans underwritten to these limits are automatically considered sound.

During construction, disbursements should not exceed actual development or construction outlays and the borrower should maintain appropriate levels of hard equity throughout the term of the loan.

Ground lease arrangements can be quite complex. Banks should engage appropriate legal counsel for the review of the lease documents before commitment (or condition commitment on their review) and the drafting of loan documentation.

Affordable Housing Loans

The OCC encourages banks to extend prudent credit to promote community development. By taking the initiative in their communities, banks may establish new markets, reinforce their identity as community institutions, and enhance their performance.

To address the needs of low-income renters, the Tax Reform Act of 1986 created incentives to develop affordable housing by offering tax credits to developers. Proceeds from the sale of these credits subsidize the development costs, thereby permitting the units to be rented at below-market rates. Nearly 90 percent of affordable housing is developed with the support of this program. Many of these projects also benefit from grants and low-interest loans from local and state government-sponsored agencies. The bank should consider this assistance in its underwriting.

Appraisers should consider the various types of financial assistance provided to affordable housing projects in estimating market value. When the benefits of such financial assistance are not appropriately reflected in a project's appraisal, the projected NOI of the project may be negatively affected, resulting in a lower market value. When this occurs, a proposed affordable housing loan may not have an LTV ratio sufficient to satisfy the standards of the agencies' real estate lending guidelines or to receive favorable treatment under the agencies' risk-based capital rules.

An appraisal of an affordable housing project should contain a market value estimate that reflects the real estate collateral and typical interests in the real estate on a cash or cash-equivalent basis. The agencies' appraisal regulations permit the appraiser to include in the market value estimate any significant financial assistance that would survive sale or foreclosure, such as the value of low-income housing tax credits (LIHTC), subsidies, and grants.

The bank should ensure that an appraiser engaged to appraise an affordable housing project is competent to perform such an appraisal, is knowledgeable about the various types of financial assistance and programs associated with affordable housing projects, and identifies and considers the effect on value of any significant amount of the financial assistance. The appraisal should contain a discussion of the value of the financial assistance that would survive sale or foreclosure and how the assistance affects the market value estimate of the project. While certain types of financial assistance, such as tenant-based rent subsidies, do not necessarily transfer to new ownership upon sale or foreclosure, the bank should ensure that the appraiser appropriately considers the effect of these items in the cash-flow analysis, when applicable.

When extending credit for an affordable housing project or purchasing the tax credits, banks should have a solid understanding of these programs and the requirements and restrictions that accompany them.[9]

Real Estate Investment Trusts

A real estate investment trust (REIT) is a tax designation for corporations that buy, develop, manage, and sell real estate assets. REITs qualify as pass-through entities that reduce or eliminate corporate income taxes so long as they conform to certain Internal Revenue Service provisions. For example, REITs are required to distribute at least 90 percent of their income to investors and must derive at least 75 percent of gross income from rents or mortgage interest. Because REITs do not pay income taxes, REIT dividends are fully taxable and as such do not qualify for the capital gains tax rate. Because REITs pay out the majority of their taxable income to investors, they are reliant on borrowing or the issuance of shares to fund expansion.

There are three major types of REITs.

- **Equity REITs** own real estate and may specialize in a specific property type, such as shopping malls or industrial properties. Alternatively, the assets may be diversified, in which case the REIT owns a mix of properties of various types. Revenues from equity REITs principally come from rental income as well as capital gains from the sale of the properties.
- **Mortgage REITs** lend mortgage money, invest in real estate-backed mortgages often purchased though mortgage originators, or purchase mortgage-backed securities. Revenue from mortgage REITs is generated primarily by the interest they earn on the mortgage loans.
- **Hybrid REITs** combine the investment strategies of equity REITs and mortgage REITs by investing in both properties and mortgages. Revenue from hybrid REITs is a combination of rental and interest income.

REIT performance can be affected by economic conditions that affect each category of specialization. For example, office REITs may be affected more by employment trends than retail REITs, although performance of each property type or geographic concentration tends to follow the general conditions of the real estate market. Thus, employment trends, interest rates, and supply and demand affect certain REITs to varying degrees.

Credit considerations in lending to REITs are similar to other types of commercial lending transactions. Before lending to a REIT, the bank should ensure that it is familiar with the

---

[9] The OCC Community Affairs Department's *Community Development Insights* "Low-Income Housing Tax Credits: Affordable Housing Investment Opportunities for Banks," February 2008, provides an overview of LIHTCs and discusses key risks and regulatory issues that should be considered for banks providing project financing as lenders or equity through the purchase of tax credits.

REIT's structure, its management, the parties to its loan agreement, any collateral, if applicable, and the quality of assets held in the REIT. REIT credits should be analyzed to determine strength of repayment sources (both cash flow and collateral adequacy), and stress testing should analyze sensitivity to changing economic conditions or under a variety of scenarios. Banks should consider borrower or tenant concentrations that may exist in the REIT's loan or equity investment portfolios.

In analyzing a loan to a REIT, operating cash flow can be measured according to a measurement known as "funds from operations" (FFO), a measure adopted to promote uniform measurement of REIT operating performance by the National Association of Real Estate Investment Trusts. FFO is sometimes used as a supplemental measure of earnings performance to net income because generally accepted accounting principles (GAAP) require that commercial property owners depreciate the cost of their properties to zero over a prescribed period of time (such as 20 years) even though the properties retain value for years in excess of that depreciation period. As such, a traditional GAAP-based measure of net income tends to overstate expenses and understate earnings.

FFO is derived by adding back depreciation and real estate amortization charges to net income and excludes gains or losses from sale of properties. While FFO measures a REIT's operating cash flow before accounting for administrative and financing expense, there may be variation in the way this measurement is computed and reported in company disclosures. For example, maintenance and repair expenses and other recurring capital expenditures may not be uniformly reflected in the FFO measure. Therefore, banks should review a company's quarterly or annual report and supplemental disclosures.

Analysis of Borrower's and Guarantor's Financial Condition

A bank should establish and maintain prudent credit underwriting practices that provide for consideration, before credit commitment, of the borrower's overall financial condition and resources, the financial responsibility of any guarantor, the nature and value of any underlying collateral, and the borrower's character and willingness to repay as agreed.

The bank should obtain appropriate financial information on the borrower(s) and guarantor(s), if applicable, including income, liquidity, cash flow, contingent liabilities, and other relevant factors. A borrower should demonstrate the capacity to meet a realistic repayment plan from available liquidity and cash flow. Cash flow from the underlying property or other indicators of borrower capacity should be evaluated to determine whether, and to what extent, the borrower can adequately service interest and principal on a prospective loan.

Cash flows should be assessed on a global basis. Global cash-flow analyses can be complex and may require integrating cash flows from business financial statements, tax returns and Schedule K-1 forms for multiple partnerships, limited liability companies (LLCs) and corporations. The analysis should consider required and discretionary cash flows from all activities and banks should understand any actual or contingent liabilities and their potential effect on repayment capacity. The analysis should focus on recurring cash flows and anticipated capital gains when income has been shown to be historically capital-gain dependent. Realistic projections of such expenses as personal debt payments, property and income taxes, and living expenses should be considered. Bank management should ensure comprehensive global cash-flow analyses are performed despite the presence of significant liquid assets, as those assets may be needed to fund other actual or contingent liabilities and other cash flow shortfalls.

When evaluating guarantor support, examiners should consider whether the guarantor has both the willingness and capacity to provide support for the credit, and whether the guarantee is legally enforceable. A presumption of willingness to provide borrower (project) support, where the guarantor has an economic incentive, is usually appropriate unless there is evidence to the contrary. Examiners should consider whether a guarantor has demonstrated his or her willingness to fulfill previous obligations, has sufficient economic incentive, and has a significant investment in the project. The bank should consider the liquidity of any assets that collateralize the guarantee. A guarantor's unpledged assets should not be considered a substitute for project equity.

Some guarantees may be limited in nature, such as interest only, construction completion only, partial principal, or stepped-down in amount or released during the loan term as certain conditions are met. The bank should closely monitor and assess the achievement of these conditions before releasing a guarantor of his or her obligation.

Loan documents should include covenants requiring the periodic submission of financial information that allows the bank to adequately monitor the borrower's and guarantor's overall financial soundness and capacity to support the credit.

Loans Secured by Owner-Occupied Properties

For owner-occupied properties, the primary source of repayment is usually the cash flow generated by the occupying business. Banks should consider the ability of the occupying business, borrower, and guarantors, if any, to repay the debt. Nevertheless, collateral-focused guidance such as SLTV and appraisals or evaluations remains relevant to the financing of these properties. Proceeds from these loans may finance the acquisition or construction of business premises or may be used for other business purposes such as working capital.

Properties such as hospitals, golf courses, recreational facilities, and car washes are considered owner-occupied unless leased to an unaffiliated party. Hotels, motels, dormitories, nursing homes, assisted-living facilities, mini-storage warehouse facilities, and similar properties are considered non-owner-occupied.

When a property is partially leased to an unaffiliated tenant, the property's classification is determined by the primary source of repayment. If 50 percent or more of the primary source of repayment is derived from third-party, unaffiliated income, the property should be considered non-owner-occupied.[10]

At times, the development of owner-occupied properties may not appear to be economically feasible. Highly specialized improvements required to meet the needs of an owner-occupant can result in a cost greater than the value that can be supported by income generated by leasing to another user. These improvements might include such features as thicker floors and higher ceilings to accommodate specialized machinery and processes. As an owner-occupied loan, the underwriting analysis should emphasize the repayment ability of the occupying business. The bank should also consider the economic value of the collateral to another user in its underwriting analysis.

In many cases, the owner of the occupying business owns the building in a separate entity and leases it to the business. Care should be taken to ensure that rents used for valuation purposes are consistent with the market to avoid relying on rental rates that have not been established in an arms-length transaction and may be inflated.

Although owner-occupied commercial properties are not included for purposes of measuring CRE concentrations as defined by supervisory guidance, a troubled credit that develops an increased reliance on collateral for repayment can contribute to a bank's CRE concentration risk.

File Documentation

12 CFR 30 (national banks) and 12 CFR 160.170 (federal savings associations), appendix A, "Interagency Guidelines for Establishing Standards for Safety and Soundness," require banks to establish and maintain loan documentation practices that

- ensure that the bank can make an informed lending decision and assess risk on an ongoing basis.
- identify the purpose and all sources of repayment for each loan and assess the ability of the borrower(s) and any guarantor(s) to repay the loan in a timely manner.
- ensure that the claims against the borrower, guarantor, security holders, and any collateral are legally enforceable.
- demonstrate appropriate administration and monitoring of the bank's loans.
- take into account the size and complexity of the bank's loans.

Documents that the bank should maintain in its files include

- an approval memorandum that documents the loan approval and provides sufficient information to approvers to permit a fully informed credit decision. The terms of the

---

[10] For more information on defining owner-occupied and non-owner-occupied properties, refer to the call report instructions, Schedule RC-C – Loans and Leases, 1.e.(1): Loans secured by owner-occupied nonfarm nonresidential properties.

loan documents must be consistent with the approval document and any subsequent amendments.

- signed financial statements for borrowers and guarantors and operating statements and rent rolls for the property, where applicable.
- a title insurance policy.
- a recorded mortgage or deed of trust securing the collateral, promissory note, lease assignments, and security agreement. The property descriptions on the mortgage or deed of trust, security agreement and assignments, title insurance policy, survey, and property tax statement must describe the same parcel.
- copies of all leases and executed tenant estoppels, insurance policies and proof of premium payment that show the bank's interest is adequately protected against hazard, liability, and, where appropriate, loss of rents and flood.
- an appropriate appraisal or evaluation and its review. The engagement letter and qualifications of the appraiser or person performing the evaluation should be included.
- property survey showing the location of the improvements on the site and any easements or encroachments.
- partnership or corporate organizational documents, borrowing resolutions and certificates of good standing, where appropriate.
- evidence that property taxes have been paid to date and that the collateral property has its own parcel identification (ID) number(s). The ID number(s) and tax parcel description must be consistent with the legal description in the collateral documents and not include other parcels that do not secure the loan. Otherwise, a parcel split is needed to sell the property, presenting a serious and possibly fatal impediment to liquidation.
- any environmental reports deemed necessary, given the location, type of project and historical use.

In addition to the above, construction loan files should contain

- a construction loan agreement describing the rights and obligations of the bank and borrower, conditions for advancing funds, repayment criteria including any mandatory principal curtailments and release prices, where appropriate, and events of default. The agreement should include a detailed budget and should identify all costs funded by the construction loan.
- information on the borrower or contractor that substantiates the expertise necessary to complete the project.
- a title insurance policy updated with each advance of funds, if such additional protection is available.
- appraisals estimating the market value of the property on an as-is and as-completed or as-stabilized basis, and stating when stabilized occupancy is expected to be achieved or sales projections for for-sale projects.
- project plans, feasibility study, and construction budget showing the development plans, project costs, marketing plans, and borrower's equity contributions. The documentation should include a detailed cost analysis for the land and hard construction costs, as well as the indirect or soft costs for the project, such as administrative costs, and architectural, engineering, and legal fees. If necessary internal expertise is not available,

a review of the construction plans and budget should be performed by an independent professional and documented in the file.

- executed construction contracts.
- soil reports.
- a foundation survey conducted after the foundation has been constructed and before further work is done to ensure that the placement of the improvements are consistent with the site plan, that the proper setback requirements are met, and that construction does not encroach on easements or adjoining property.
- a completion and payment bond.
- builder's risk insurance.

Documentation files for tract development loans frequently contain a master note for the gross amount of the loan for the entire project and a master mortgage or deed of trust covering all of the land involved in the project. The files should include an appraisal for the tract development as well as an individual model appraisal for each type of house to be built. The appraisal should also include a market analysis for the entire development that provides an estimated rate of absorption. The appraisal should indicate that the homes to be constructed are in sufficient demand, given the project's location, unit styles, and unit sales price.

A developer also might seek confirmation from the U.S. Department of Housing and Urban Development's Federal Housing Administration (FHA) and the U.S. Department of Veterans Affairs (VA) that the tract development meets the FHA and VA building standards. This allows the developer to market the homes to individuals who wish to obtain mortgages through the FHA or VA mortgage insurance programs.

Appraisals and Evaluations

12 CFR 34, subpart C–Appraisals (national banks) and 12 CFR 164 (federal savings associations) specify which transactions require the services of an appraiser and whether the appraiser must be state-certified or state-licensed. These regulations also prescribe minimum appraisal standards, requirements for appraiser independence, and competency. OCC Bulletin 2010-42, "Sound Practices for Appraisals and Evaluations: Interagency Appraisal and Evaluation Guidelines," describes supervisory expectations for real estate appraisals and evaluations and provides clarification on the OCC's expectations for prudent appraisal and evaluation policies, procedures, and practices. The OCC may require an appraisal or evaluation whenever the agency believes it is necessary to address safety and soundness concerns.

While valuations are generally required for almost all real-estate related transactions secured by real estate,[11] the appraisal regulations permit the use of evaluations in lieu of appraisals for transactions

---

[11] 12 CFR 34, subpart C–Appraisals (national banks) and 12 CFR 164 (federal savings associations) exempts certain other transactions from the requirements for an appraisal or evaluation such as where a loan is guaranteed by the federal government or a federal agency. See the regulations and OCC Bulletin 2010-42,

- where the loan amount is $250,000 or less,
- where the transaction is a business loan of $1 million or less and income from the sale or rental of real estate[12] is not the primary source of repayment,
- for loans representing an existing extension of credit where there is no new money advanced other than to cover reasonable closing costs, or
- for loans representing an existing extension of credit where new money is advanced, provided there has been no obvious and material change in market conditions or the physical aspects of the property that would threaten the adequacy of the collateral.

The services of a state-certified appraiser are required for

- all loans or other transactions of $1 million or more,
- nonresidential loans or other transactions of $250,000 or more, other than those involving one- to four-family properties, or
- complex residential loans or other transactions of $250,000 or more.

For all other real-estate related loans or transactions, appraisals may be performed by either state-certified or state-licensed appraisers.

For transactions requiring an appraisal or evaluation, if a bank has a valid and compliant appraisal or evaluation that was previously obtained in connection with the real estate loan, the bank does not need to obtain a new appraisal or evaluation to comply with these regulations. OCC Bulletin 2010-42, "Sound Practices for Appraisals and Evaluations: Interagency Appraisal and Evaluation Guidelines" (see section XIV, "Validity of Appraisals and Evaluations"), states that banks should establish criteria for assessing whether an existing appraisal or evaluation remains valid and discusses factors that should be considered, such as

- passage of time.
- volatility of the local market.
- changes in terms and availability of financing.
- natural disasters.
- limited or over supply of competing properties.
- improvements to the subject property or competing properties.
- lack of maintenance of the subject or competing properties.
- changes in underlying economic and market assumptions, such as capitalization rates and lease terms.
- changes in zoning, building materials, or technology.
- environmental contamination.

"Sound Practices for Appraisals and Evaluations: Interagency Appraisal and Evaluation Guidelines," for a full description of exempted transactions.

[12] The term "real estate" as used here includes any real estate and is not limited to the property that collateralizes the loan.

The application of an arbitrary period of time, such as 12 months, should not be used as stand-alone criteria for determining the validity of an appraisal or an evaluation. The passage of time is just one component of that assessment and other factors that affect value must be considered in making such a determination. The bank should maintain documentation that provides the facts and analysis used to support the institution's conclusion that an existing appraisal or evaluation remains valid and may continue to be used in support of the property's market value.

A bank may take a lien on real estate without obtaining an appraisal or evaluation if the lien is taken in an abundance of caution. To qualify for this exemption, the extension of credit must be well supported by the borrower's cash flow or other collateral. The bank should verify and document the adequacy and reliability of these repayment sources and conclude that knowing the market value of the real estate is unnecessary to support the credit decision. This exemption does not apply if the transaction would not be adequately secured by sources of repayment other than the real estate, even if the contributory value of the real estate collateral is low relative to the entire collateral pool and other repayment sources. See OCC Bulletin 2010-42, "Sound Practices for Appraisals and Evaluations: Interagency Appraisal and Evaluation Guidelines," for a more complete discussion.

Appraisal and Evaluation Program

OCC Bulletin 2010-42, "Sound Practices for Appraisals and Evaluations: Interagency Appraisal and Evaluation Guidelines," states that the bank's real estate appraisal and evaluation policies and procedures should be reviewed as part of the examination of the bank's overall real estate-related activities.

Independence of the appraisal function is critical to an effective valuation program. The appraisal function must be isolated from influence by the loan production and collection staff and have independent reporting lines. Small banks where this independence is not achievable should clearly demonstrate that they have prudent safeguards in place that isolate their valuation programs from influence or interference from the loan production process.

Communication between the bank's valuation staff and the appraiser or person performing the evaluation is essential for conveying information about the bank's policies and procedures. The bank may ask the appraiser to consider additional information about the subject property or about comparable properties, provide additional supporting information about the basis for a valuation, or correct factual errors in an appraisal. The bank must not directly or indirectly coerce, influence, or otherwise encourage an appraiser or a person who performs an evaluation to misstate or misrepresent the property's value. Inappropriate communication includes

- communicating a predetermined, expected, or qualifying estimate of value or a loan amount or target LTV ratio to an appraiser or person performing an evaluation.
- specifying a minimum value requirement for the property that is needed to approve the loan or as a condition of ordering the valuation.
- conditioning a person's compensation on loan consummation.

- failing to compensate a person because a property is not valued at a certain amount.
- implying that current or future retention of a person's services depends on the amount at which the appraiser or person performing an evaluation values a property.
- excluding a person from consideration for future engagement because a property's reported market value does not meet a specified threshold.

The bank's policies and procedures should specify methods for communication that ensure independence in the collateral valuation function.

The selection and engagement of a competent, qualified and independent appraiser for each assignment is a regulatory requirement and a prudent business practice. The bank should establish standards for the independent selection, evaluation, and monitoring of appraisers or persons performing evaluations.

The bank's use of a borrower-ordered or borrower-provided appraisal violates the agencies' appraisal regulations. A borrower can, however, inform the bank that a current appraisal exists, and the bank may request it directly from the financial services institution that commissioned it. The bank is permitted to rely on an appraisal performed for another financial services institution, provided (1) the appraiser was selected and engaged by the institution transferring the appraisal, (2) the appraiser had no direct or indirect, financial or otherwise, interest in the property or parties to the transaction, (3) the bank determines that the appraisal remains valid, (4) the bank determines that the appraisal conforms to OCC appraisal requirements and guidelines, and (5) the appraisal is otherwise appropriate for the transaction. A bank should perform a more thorough review of the appraisal when accepting an appraisal from another financial services institution to confirm that the appraisal complies with the regulation and has sufficient information to support the lending decision. Further, the regulated institution accepting the appraisal should determine whether appropriate documentation is available to confirm that the financial services institution (not the borrower) ordered the appraisal.

Banks should establish procedures for selecting and approving appraisers and procedures for monitoring appraiser performance. If the bank uses an approved appraiser list, the procedures should include a process for qualifying an appraiser for initial placement on the list and periodic monitoring of the appraiser's performance and credentials to assess whether to retain the appraiser on the list. The bank should establish procedures governing the removal of an appraiser from the list and should ensure that appraisers are not removed for reasons that serve to diminish appraiser independence. The list's use should be reviewed periodically to confirm that effective procedures and controls are in place to ensure independence in the list's development, administration, and maintenance.

The bank should use written engagement letters when ordering appraisals. The letters should identify the client and intended use and user(s), as defined in the Uniform Standards of Professional Appraisal Practice (USPAP) and also may specify whether there are any legal or contractual restrictions on the sharing of the appraisal with other parties. The bank should include engagement letters in its credit file. To avoid the appearance of conflict of interest, the appraiser or person performing the evaluation should not begin work on the assignment until he or she has been engaged.

Appraisal and Evaluation Reviews

Reviews of appraisals and evaluations should determine whether the methods, assumptions, and value conclusions are reasonable. The review should determine whether the appraisal or evaluation complies with the appraisal regulations and supervisory guidelines, as well as the bank's policies, and address whether the appraisal contains sufficient information and analysis on which to base a sound credit decision.

Banks should establish qualification criteria for persons who are eligible to review appraisals and evaluations. Persons who review appraisals and evaluations should be independent of the transaction and have no direct or indirect interest, financial or otherwise, in the property or transaction, and be independent of and insulated from any influence by loan production staff. Small or rural institutions or branches with limited staff should implement prudent safeguards for reviewing appraisals and evaluations when absolute lines of independence cannot be achieved. Reviewers should possess the requisite education, expertise, and competence to perform the review commensurate with the complexity of the transaction, type of real property, and market.

Banks should implement a risk-focused approach for determining the depth of the review needed to ensure that appraisals and evaluations contain sufficient information and analysis to support the institution's decision to engage in the transaction.

Section XV, "Reviewing Appraisals and Evaluations" of OCC Bulletin 2010-42, "Sound Practices for Appraisals and Evaluations: Interagency Appraisal and Evaluation Guidelines" provides additional guidance.

CRE Concentrations of Credit

Several key pieces of supervisory guidance provide bankers and examiners a framework for the management of CRE credit concentrations.

The *Comptroller's Handbook* booklet "Concentrations of Credit" renews emphasis on stress testing as a tool to identify and quantify concentration risks and enhances the definition of a credit concentration to encourage qualitative considerations in addition to absolute dollar amounts. The booklet addresses risk management, stress testing, and capital planning aspects of concentration management.

OCC Bulletin 2006-46, "Concentrations in Commercial Real Estate Lending, Sound Risk Management Practices: Interagency Guidance on CRE Concentration Risk Management," reminds banks that strong risk-management practices and appropriate levels of capital are important elements of a sound CRE lending program, particularly when the bank has a concentration in CRE loans. The guidance reinforces and enhances the agencies' existing regulations and guidelines for real estate lending and loan portfolio management.

OCC Bulletin 2012-16, "Capital Planning: Guidance for Evaluating Capital Planning and Adequacy," explains supervisory expectations regarding capital adequacy and, in addition to providing guidance on capital planning, addresses risk management and stress testing. It emphasizes the importance of a forward-looking strategic focus to identify vulnerabilities that could be posed by current or planned concentrations and to assess their effect on capital.

The primary source of revenue for most banks is the extension of credit. The bank's credit activities, when prudently measured, monitored, and controlled, benefit shareholders, customers, and the communities served. Flawed or shortsighted credit risk management practices, including excessive and unmanaged CRE concentrations, have been key factors in banking crises and failures. Effective portfolio risk management must encompass the management of loan concentrations whose collective performance has the potential to negatively affect the bank even though each individual transaction within a concentration may be soundly underwritten.

When a pool of CRE loans is sensitive to the same economic, financial, or business development factors, that sensitivity, if triggered, may cause the sum of the transactions to perform as if it were a single, large exposure. History shows that concentrations in CRE lending coupled with depressed CRE markets contribute to significant credit losses, even where underwriting practices are strong. It is important that the bank's risk-management practices are commensurate with the risk profile of the bank and continue to evolve with increasing CRE concentrations.

Banks are encouraged to stratify their CRE portfolios into segments that reflect common sensitivities for purposes of identifying concentrations. For example, the bank may segment its CRE portfolio by property type, geographic market, tenant concentrations, tenant industries, developer concentrations, and risk rating. Other useful stratifications may include loan structure, loan purpose, LTV, debt-service coverage, policy exceptions on newly underwritten credit facilities, and affiliated loans.

Management should regularly evaluate the degree of correlation between related real estate segments and establish internal lending guidelines and concentration limits that control the bank's overall risk exposure. Additionally, appropriate strategies for managing CRE concentration levels, including a contingency plan to reduce or mitigate concentrations in the event of adverse CRE market conditions, should be developed.

The sophistication of a bank's CRE risk management processes should be appropriate for the size of the portfolio, as well as the level and nature of concentrations and the associated risk to the bank.

Key Elements for Risk Management of CRE Loan Concentrations

OCC Bulletin 2006-46, "Concentrations in Commercial Real Estate Lending, Sound Risk Management Practices: Interagency Guidance on CRE Concentration Risk Management," states that banks should address the following key elements in establishing a risk-management framework for CRE concentration of credit risk.

Board and Management Oversight

The board is responsible for establishing effective policy guidelines and approving the overall CRE lending strategy. The board must remain informed of the level of risk posed by CRE concentrations and ensure management implements appropriate procedures and controls to operate within board approved policies, concentration limits, and lending strategies.

Portfolio Management

As previously noted, management's ability to understand and evaluate CRE exposures at the portfolio level is critical to effective portfolio management and contingency planning.

Management Information Systems

The sophistication of MIS necessarily varies with the complexity of the CRE portfolio and the level and nature of concentration risk. Regardless of sophistication, MIS should provide management with timely and sufficient information to identify, measure, monitor, and control CRE concentration risk.

For banks with significant concentrations, management needs comprehensive data, including both on- and off-balance-sheet credit exposures, to segment a portfolio and facilitate risk diversification. Different user groups (lending management, credit administration, senior management, etc.) require different types of portfolio information to function effectively. Systems' architecture should provide both loan-level detail and aggregate information in a standardized reporting format, as well as offer ad-hoc reporting functionality.

Banks with high CRE concentrations should have strong concentration management systems. It is the board's responsibility to establish prudent concentration limits that adequately segment credit exposures into sufficiently granular portions; then it is bank management's job to develop the monitoring and control systems to manage the concentration risk. Concentration reports should contain sufficient detail to adequately segment the portfolio by product type, geography (for banks that make loans in multiple geographies), etc. Meaningful concentration analysis requires accurate and consistent loan and collateral coding.

Market Analysis

Management should perform periodic market analyses for the various property types and geographic markets represented in the CRE portfolio. The sophistication of the analysis varies depending on the bank's relative exposure, market share, and the availability of market data. Although less data may be available in smaller markets management should be able to demonstrate an understanding of the economic and business factors influencing the bank's lending area.

Credit Underwriting Standards

Underwriting standards should be clear, measurable, and reflect the level of risk acceptable to the board of directors. CRE lending policies should address the underwriting standards outlined in the "Underwriting Standards" section of this booklet. Credit analysis should focus on the borrower's creditworthiness and project-specific considerations, as appropriate.

Portfolio Stress Testing and Sensitivity Analysis

Banks with CRE concentrations should perform portfolio level stress tests or sensitivity analysis on a regular basis. The following issuances provide guidance related to stress testing.

The OCC issued bulletin 2012-14, "Stress Testing: Interagency Stress Testing Guidance," for banking organizations with total consolidated assets of more than $10 billion. The guidance outlines general principles for a satisfactory stress testing framework and describes various stress testing approaches and how stress testing should be used at various levels within an organization.

OCC Bulletin 2012-33, "Community Bank Stress Testing: Supervisory Guidance," provides guidance to national banks and federal savings associations with $10 billion or less in total assets on using stress testing to identify and quantify risk in loan portfolios and help establish effective strategic and capital planning processes. The bulletin discusses various stress testing methods and approaches.

In conjunction with the release of OCC Bulletin 2012-33, the OCC issued a "Portfolio Stress Test Tool for Income Producing Commercial Real Estate," which is available to banks on BankNet, the OCC's secure Web site for communicating with national banks and federal savings associations. The Microsoft Excel-based tool provides banks and examiners with a straightforward and accessible method of evaluating the potential effect of the bank's CRE loan portfolio on the bank's condition in a stressed environment. While use of the tool is optional, all banks are expected to have the ability to analyze the effect of adverse economic events on their financial condition. Examiners may access the tool and examiner guidance on its use in the Midsize and Community Bank Supervision (MCBS) Supervisory Information portal on the OCC's intranet.

The sophistication of stress testing should consider the complexity and risk characteristics of the CRE portfolio. Banks should consider stress testing not only at the transaction level during underwriting and as a function of ongoing credit monitoring, but also at the portfolio level where significant concentrations exist. The objective of portfolio level stress testing should be to quantify the effect of changing economic conditions on asset quality, earnings, and capital, and to identify potential exposures to external events.

The analysis should focus on the more vulnerable segments of the bank's CRE portfolio, taking into consideration the prevailing market environment and the bank's business strategy. For example, banks with concentrations in income-producing properties should consider, as applicable, the effect of changes in interest rates, vacancy rates, lease rates, and expenses on the portfolio's overall performance. Analysis of construction and development portfolios may include similar variables but should also consider testing for unique risks, such as the effect from various absorption scenarios, changes in sales prices, and cost overruns.

Banks with large and complex portfolios may utilize more sophisticated financial models that stress probability of default and loss given default. At smaller, less complex banks, management can often review a limited number of the largest credits or use statistical techniques to extrapolate results across portfolios. For example, the bank could evaluate the effect of declining office space rental rates on a meaningful sample of loans to determine at what rental rate the projects could no longer service debt. The results of the sample could be aggregated and applied across the portfolio to identify the volume of the portfolio subject to a decline, e.g., 10 percent, in rental rates.

Management should maintain documentation of the stress testing program and reevaluate the results periodically. Conclusions from stress testing should be integrated into the bank's risk management program and planning functions. Management should use the results to evaluate whether performance under stressed conditions is within the bank's board of directors' risk tolerance, whether policies and procedures are appropriate, and if strategic and capital plans remain reasonable.

Credit Risk Review Function

A strong credit risk review function is an integral tool used to assist management's self-assessment of CRE concentrations and emerging risks. The foundation of the bank's credit risk review function is an effective, accurate, and timely risk-rating system. Risk ratings should be risk sensitive, objective, and reviewed regularly for appropriateness. Additional discussion can be found in the "Loan Review" section of this booklet.

Supervisory Review of CRE Concentrations and Risk Management

While guidance does not establish specific CRE lending limits, OCC Bulletin 2006-46, "Concentrations in Commercial Real Estate Lending, Sound Risk Management Practices: Interagency Guidance on CRE Concentration Risk Management," describes criteria that, when approached or exceeded, may prompt further supervisory analysis of the level, nature, and management of a bank's CRE concentration risk:

(1) Total reported loans for construction, land development, and other land[13] represent 100 percent or more of the bank's total capital;[14] or

(2) Total non-owner-occupied CRE loans[15] represent 300 percent or more of the bank's total capital, and the outstanding balance of the bank's CRE loan portfolio has increased by 50 percent.

The effectiveness of a bank's risk management practices is a key component of the supervisory evaluation of a bank's CRE concentrations. Examiners will discuss concentrations with management to assess CRE exposure levels and risk management practices. Banks that have experienced recent, significant growth in CRE lending will receive closer supervisory review.

Examiners are reminded that, as with other concentrations, CRE concentrations should be reported on the "Concentrations" page of the Report of Examination (ROE) when these concentrations pose challenges to management or present unusual or significant risk to the bank. A historical analysis demonstrates a significantly increased risk of failure among banks that have exceeded the thresholds described above.[16] CRE concentrations of credit approaching or exceeding these thresholds should be reported on the "Concentrations" page of the ROE and any supervisory concerns regarding such concentrations of credit should be discussed in other appropriate narrative sections of the ROE.

When evaluating CRE concentrations, examiners consider a bank's own analysis of its CRE portfolio, including consideration of such factors as

- portfolio diversification across property types.
- geographic dispersion of CRE loans.
- underwriting standards.
- level of presold units or other types of take-out commitments on construction loans.
- portfolio liquidity (ability to sell or securitize exposures on the secondary market).

While consideration of these factors should not change the method of identifying a credit concentration, these factors may mitigate the risk posed by the concentration.

---

[13] As reported in the call report FFIEC 031 and 041, schedule RC–C—Loans and Lease Financing Receivables part I, item lal.a. and Memorandum item 3.

[14] For purposes of this guidance, the term "total capital" means the total risk-based capital as reported in the call report FFIEC 031 and 041, schedule RC–R—Regulatory Capital, item 21.

[15] As reported in the call report FFIEC 031 and 041, schedule RC–C, part I, items 1a, 1d, 1e(1.a., 1.d., 1.e.(2), and Memorandum item 3.

[16] *An Analysis of the Impact of the Commercial Real Estate Concentration Guidance,* OCC and Federal Reserve Joint Study, April 2013.

Environmental Risk Management

Environmental contamination may negatively affect the value of real property collateral as well as create potential liability for the bank under various environmental laws. Therefore, the bank's loan policy should establish a program for assessing the potential adverse effect of environmental contamination and ensure appropriate controls to limit the bank's exposure to environmental liability associated with real estate taken as collateral.

The Comprehensive Environmental Response, Compensation, and Liability Act of 1980 (CERCLA), also known as Superfund, was enacted to address abandoned hazardous waste sites in the United States. The law has subsequently been amended by the Superfund Amendments and Reauthorization Act of 1986 (SARA) and the Small Business Liability Relief and Brownfields Revitalization Act of 2002. Under CERCLA, the U.S. Environmental Protection Agency (EPA) is charged with identifying contaminated property, finding the parties responsible for the contaminated property, and requiring the parties to either cleanup the property or reimburse EPA for its cleanup In addition to federal laws, states have their own environmental laws. Lenders should be familiar with the laws in their market areas.

The EPA's All Appropriate Inquiry Final Rule (AAI), issued in 2006, establishes standards for due diligence that can allow a property owner to qualify for defenses to liability under CERCLA and some state laws. This rule created new standards (ASTM E1527-05)[17] for what is commonly known as a "Phase I" environmental assessment.

Banks that hold mortgages on property as secured lenders are exempt from CERCLA liability if certain criteria are met. CERCLA section 101(20) contains a secured creditor exemption that eliminates owner/operator liability for lenders who hold ownership in a CERCLA facility primarily to protect their security interest in the facility, provided they do not "participate in the management of the facility." Generally, "participation in the management" may apply if a bank exercises decision-making control over a property's environmental compliance or exercises control at a level similar to that enjoyed by a manager of the facility or property. "Participation in management" does *not* include such actions as property inspections, requiring a response action to be taken to address contamination, providing financial advice, or renegotiating or restructuring the terms of the security interest. In addition, the secured creditor exemption provides that simply foreclosing on a property does not result in liability for a bank, provided the bank takes "reasonable steps" to divest itself of the property "at the earliest practicable, commercially reasonable time, on commercially reasonable terms." Generally, a bank may maintain business activities and close down operations at a property, so long as the property is listed for sale shortly after the foreclosure date or at the earliest practicable, commercially reasonable time.

While these exemptions may limit a lender's liability for cleanup, they do not protect the lender from the decline in value that contamination can cause due to the cost of remediation that may have to be undertaken by the bank or a prospective purchaser or the stigma associated with a contaminated property. Further, it does not protect a responsible borrower

---

[17] Standard established by ASTM International, formerly known as the American Society for Testing and Materials.

from liability for cleanup, the cost of which may severely impair the borrower's ability to repay the loan. For these reasons, a bank should perform an evaluation of the borrower's or tenant's business activities and any property taken as collateral before funding a loan and before taking title in satisfaction of debt. The evaluation should be commensurate with the risk of loss that collateral contamination or borrower liability poses to the bank. While the lender's exemption from liability under CERCLA does not require that the evaluation meet the standards under AAI, an AAI-compliant study can provide the best assessment of a property's environmental condition, potential liability for a borrower, and disposition strategies upon foreclosure.

An appropriate environmental risk management program should reflect the level and nature of the bank's real estate lending activities, its risk profile, and consideration of applicable environmental laws. The program should be reviewed and approved with its lending policies annually by the bank's board of directors or a designated committee of the board.

In adopting an effective environmental risk management program, the bank should

- develop policies and procedures that reflect potential environmental risks associated with lending in markets and to industries served by the bank. Procedures should clearly specify the bank's requirements for determining potential environmental concerns. For example, procedures should include guidelines that the lending staff should follow in conducting an initial analysis of potential environmental impact. Procedures should also specify the circumstances in which a more detailed environmental assessment, such as an AAI-compliant evaluation, should be conducted by a qualified professional.
- provide for the receipt and evaluation of environmental risk assessment reports before the bank's final commitment to lend on a transaction.
- establish procedures for assessing environmental concerns associated with assets before acquisition by the bank in workout or foreclosures as well as the bank's investment in real estate assets for its own use.
- ensure that persons responsible for evaluating environmental risk possess relevant knowledge, skill, and competence. The bank's program should specify selection criteria to evaluate and monitor the performance of third-party professionals, such as environmental experts or legal counsel, who may be consulted to assess environmental risk (see next section on "Environmental Legislation").
- provide guidelines that the lending staff should follow for monitoring potential environmental concerns for the duration of loans held in the bank's loan portfolio. These guidelines should focus on changes in business activities that might result in an increased risk of environmental contamination associated with the property, thus adversely affecting the value of the collateral.
- maintain guidelines for loan documentation that protect the bank from environmental liability and related losses. Loan documentation should ensure that contractual provisions, including rights of access, are sufficient to facilitate AAI-compliant evaluations.A bank's policies and procedures should reflect adequate consideration of the EPA's AAI rule. Such a policy should incorporate certain key elements, including
- an analysis of current environmental laws and due diligence requirements for borrowers and the bank.

- a level of due diligence internally required in all real estate loan transactions.
- risk thresholds based on property type, use and loan amount for determining when and what type of due diligence is required.
- varying due diligence methods depending on the type of loan, the amount of the loan and the risk category, including borrower questionnaire or screening, site visit, government records review, historical records review, testing or inspections using qualified professionals.
- the potential for significant impact resulting from the presence of hazardous building material such as asbestos and lead-based paint.
- appraisal requirements for disclosing and taking into consideration any environmental risk factors.
- criteria for evaluating environmental risk factors and costs in the loan approval process.
- criteria for determining the circumstances in which the bank would normally decline loan requests based on environmental factors.
- environmental provisions for incorporation into transaction documentation:
    - for commitment letters: extent of due diligence required, borrower costs, approval contingencies, reporting obligations, documentation requirements, etc.
    - for loan documentation: representations and warranties, inspection requirements, reporting requirements, lien covenants, indemnification provisions, and provisions allowing for the acceleration of the loan, refusal to extend funds under a line of credit, or exercise other remedies in the event of foreclosure.
- collateral monitoring and periodic inspection requirements throughout the loan term for properties with higher environmental risk.
- a means of evaluating potential environmental liability risk and environmental factors that could impact the ability to recover loan funds in the event of a foreclosure.
- guidelines for maintaining lender liability exemptions, avoiding owner/operator liability, and for qualifying for Landowner Liability Protections under CERCLA and AAI if the bank acquires ownership of the property.

Risk Rating CRE Loans

Banks are expected to maintain credit risk-management systems that produce accurate and timely risk ratings. Early and accurate risk identification is critical to ensuring problem loans are identified in a timely manner. This enhances flexibility in troubled loan resolution, contributes to the timely recognition of losses, and enables the maintenance of an appropriate ALLL balance. Credit risk ratings should be reviewed and updated whenever relevant new information is received. OCC Bulletin 2009-32, "Commercial Real Estate (CRE) Loans: Guidance on Prudent CRE Loan Workouts," provides interagency guidance on the risk rating of CRE loans.

Analyzing Repayment Capacity of the Borrower

The primary focus of an examiner's review of a commercial loan and binding commitments is the borrower's ability to repay the loan. The major factors that influence this review are the borrower's willingness and capacity to repay the loan under reasonable terms and the cash flow potential of the underlying collateral or business.

When analyzing a commercial borrower's repayment ability, examiners should consider the following factors:

- Character, overall financial condition, resources, and payment record of the borrower.
- Nature and degree of protection provided by the cash flow from business operations, or the collateral on a global basis that considers the borrower's total debt obligations.
- Market conditions that may influence repayment prospects and the cash flow potential of the business operations or underlying collateral.
- Prospects for repayment support from any financially responsible guarantors.

Evaluating Guarantees

The presence of a guarantee from a financially responsible guarantor may improve the prospects for repayment of the debt obligation and may be sufficient to preclude classification or reduce the severity of classification. The attributes of a financially responsible guarantor include the following.

- The guarantor has both the financial capacity and willingness to provide support for the credit through ongoing payments, curtailments or re-margining.
- The guarantee is adequate to provide support for repayment of the indebtedness, in whole or in part, during the remaining loan term.
- The guarantee is written and legally enforceable.

The bank should have sufficient information on the guarantor's global financial condition, income, liquidity, cash flow, contingent liabilities, and other relevant factors (including credit ratings, when available) to demonstrate the guarantor's financial capacity to fulfill the obligation. This assessment includes consideration of the total number and amount of guarantees currently extended by a guarantor in order to assess whether the guarantor has the financial capacity to fulfill the contingent claims that exist.

Examiners should consider whether a guarantor has demonstrated its willingness to fulfill all current and previous obligations, has sufficient economic incentive, and has a significant investment in the project. An important consideration is whether previously required performance under guarantees was voluntary or the result of legal or other actions by the lender to enforce the guarantee.

Assessing Collateral Values

When reviewing the reasonableness of the facts and assumptions associated with the value of an income-producing property, examiners should evaluate

- current and projected vacancy and absorption rates.
- lease renewal trends and anticipated rents.
- effective rental rates or sale prices, considering sales and financing concessions.
- time frame for achieving stabilized occupancy or sellout.
- volume and trends in past due leases.
- NOI of the property as compared with budget projections, reflecting reasonable operating and maintenance costs.
- discount rates and direct capitalization rates.

Assumptions, when recently made by qualified appraisers (and, as appropriate, by the bank) and when consistent with the discussion above, should be given a reasonable amount of deference by examiners. Examiners also should use the appropriate market-value conclusion in their collateral assessments. For example, when the bank plans to provide the resources to complete a project, examiners may consider the project's prospective market value in the computation of the committed loan amount in their analysis.

Examiners generally are not expected to challenge the underlying valuation assumptions, including discount rates and capitalization rates, used in appraisals or evaluations when these assumptions differ only in a limited way from norms that would generally be associated with the collateral under review. The estimated value of the underlying collateral may be adjusted for credit analysis purposes when the examiner can establish that any underlying facts or assumptions are inappropriate or can support alternative assumptions.

Many CRE borrowers may have other indebtedness secured by other business assets, such as furniture, fixtures, equipment, inventory, and accounts receivable. For these commercial loans, the bank should have appropriate policies and practices for quantifying the value of such assets, determining the acceptability of the collateral, and perfecting its security interest. The bank also should have appropriate procedures for ongoing monitoring of the value of its collateral interests and security protection.

Other Considerations

Changing economic conditions can have a significant effect on the performance of CRE portfolios. Factors such as changes or imbalances in supply and demand can significantly influence a number of variables from vacancy and rental rates to the value of properties. For these reasons, bankers and examiners should understand current and projected economic conditions, particularly within the bank's lending area, and the potential effect to the bank from changing economic conditions.

Timely payments are not, by themselves, a reliable indicator of the health of a credit. A troubled borrower often makes debt-service payments his or her highest priority and may divert funds required to pay real estate taxes, maintenance, vendors, and other expenses to meet his or her debt obligations. Rather than being an early indicator of distress, late or missed payments may not occur until a credit has already experienced significant deterioration.

Close monitoring to allow timely recognition of potential issues and the ability to recognize and anticipate financial difficulties are important tools in effectively controlling risk. Warning indicators can include the following:

- Delinquent real estate taxes.
- Declining sales prices or rental rates.
- Cancellations in sales contracts or reservations.
- Liberal sales or unusually generous concessions including rent, tenant improvement allowances, moving allowances, and lease buyouts.
- Slower absorption of space in new projects than anticipated.
- Delinquent lease payments from major tenants.
- Higher vacancy and turnover rates.
- Changes to the initial concept or development plan (for example, a condominium construction project converts to an apartment project).
- Construction budget overruns and borrower requests for significant reallocation of funds to other budget line items.
- Late or delinquent payments.
- Draw requests ahead of schedule for work yet to be completed.
- Construction delays or other unanticipated events that could lead to cost overruns.
- Liens due to worker or supplier payment disputes.
- Borrower requests for additional financing due to unanticipated costs or expenses.
- Deterioration in the performance of the borrower's other properties or businesses.
- Interest reserves that have been repacked.

Underwriting can also reflect changing market conditions. Increasingly liberal underwriting can be a response to increased competition among banks for loans or a weakening borrower base. The following are some examples of underwriting weaknesses that may be indicative of credit deterioration and increasing credit risk.

- Liberally underwritten loans that fail to take stressed market conditions into account.
- Loans with limited hard equity contributions by the borrower.
- Loans on speculative undeveloped property for which the only source of repayment is sale of the property.
- Loans for commercial development projects without significant preleasing or presales commitments, or where prospects for permanent financing are compromised.
- Loans to borrowers with development plans that are not viable because of changes in market conditions.
- Appraisals that contain market analyses or feasibility studies that reflect unrealistic assumptions relative to current market conditions.
- Failure to require principal curtailments when appropriate.
- Loans that are renewed on an interest-only basis.
- Rewrites or renewals for the sole purpose of deferring maturity.

Although the magnitude of economic changes can be difficult to predict, management's ability to recognize early warning signs, understand credit risk, and plan for changing market conditions can be the difference between a bank's successful weathering of economic turmoil and failing.

Classification of CRE Loans

As with other types of loans, CRE loans that are adequately protected by the current sound worth and debt service capacity of the borrower, guarantor, or the underlying collateral generally should not be classified. Similarly, loans to sound borrowers that are refinanced or renewed in accordance with prudent underwriting standards should not be classified or criticized unless well-defined weaknesses exist that jeopardize repayment. Further, loans should not be adversely classified solely because the borrower is associated with a particular industry that is experiencing financial difficulties or because the collateral has declined in value.

When the bank's restructurings are not supported by adequate analysis and documentation, examiners are expected to exercise reasonable judgment in reviewing and determining loan classifications until the bank is able to provide information to support management's conclusions and internal loan grades.

Special Mention

A special mention asset has potential weaknesses that deserve management's close attention. If left uncorrected, these potential weaknesses may result in deterioration of the repayment prospects for the asset or in the bank's credit position at some future date. Special mention assets are not adversely classified and do not expose the bank to sufficient risk to warrant adverse classification.

Potential weaknesses in CRE loans may include construction delays, changes in concept or project plan, slow leasing, rental concessions, deteriorating market conditions, impending expiry of a major lease, or other adverse events that do not currently jeopardize repayment.

Such loans require an elevated level of monitoring.

Substandard

A substandard asset is inadequately protected by the current sound worth and paying capacity of the obligor or of the collateral pledged, if any. Assets so classified must have a well-defined weakness or weaknesses that jeopardize the liquidation of the debt. Substandard assets are characterized by the distinct possibility that the bank will sustain some loss if the deficiencies are not corrected.

Well-defined weaknesses in a CRE loan may include

- slower than projected leasing or sales activity that threatens to result in protracted repayment or default.
- lower than projected lease rates or sales prices that jeopardize repayment capacity.
- changes in concept or plan due to unfavorable market conditions.
- construction or tax liens.
- inability to obtain necessary zoning or permits necessary to develop the project as planned.
- diversion of needed cash from an otherwise viable property to satisfy the demands of a troubled borrower or guarantor.
- material imbalances in the construction budget.
- significant construction delays.
- expiration of a major lease or default by a major tenant.
- poorly structured or overly liberal repayment terms.

Although substandard assets exhibit loss potential in the aggregate, an individual substandard asset may not (e.g., because of adequate collateral coverage). If full collection of both interest and principal is in doubt, the loan should be placed on nonaccrual.

When a project has slowed or stalled and the guarantor is providing some support but the loan has not been restructured, unless the guarantor is providing support of principal payments sufficient to retire the debt under reasonable terms, a substandard classification is typically warranted. If the guarantor is keeping interest payments current and shows a documented willingness and capacity to do so in the future, and collateral values protect against loss, the loan should generally be left on accrual. This level of support, however, does not fully mitigate the well-defined weaknesses in the credit and does not preclude a substandard classification.

Doubtful

An asset classified as doubtful has all the weaknesses inherent in one classified "substandard" with the added characteristic that the weaknesses make collection or liquidation in full, on the basis of currently existing facts, conditions, and values, highly questionable and improbable.

The amount of the loan balance in excess of the fair value of the real estate collateral, or portions thereof, can be adversely classified as doubtful when the exposure may be affected by the outcomes of certain pending events and the amount of the loss cannot be reasonably determined. If warranted by the underlying circumstances, an examiner may use a doubtful classification on the entire loan balance. Examiners should, however, use a doubtful classification infrequently and for a limited time period to permit the pending events to be resolved. Circumstances that might warrant a doubtful classification for CRE loans could include collateral values that are uncertain due to a lack of comparables in an inactive market, impending changes such as zoning classification, environmental issues, or the pending resolution of legal issues that may affect the realization of value in a sale.

Loss

Assets classified as a loss are considered uncollectible and of such little value that their continuance as bankable assets is not warranted. This classification does not mean that the asset has absolutely no recovery or salvage value, but rather that it is not practical or desirable to defer writing off this basically worthless asset even though partial recovery may be realized in the future.

As a general classification principle, for a troubled CRE loan that is dependent on the operation or the sale of collateral for repayment, any portion of the loan balance that exceeds the amount that is adequately secured by the market value of the real estate collateral less costs to sell should be classified as a loss if that portion of the loan balance amount is deemed uncollectible. This principle applies when repayment of the debt is provided solely by the underlying real estate collateral and when there are no other available and reliable sources of repayment.

For additional guidance on the classification of real estate loans, consult OCC Bulletin 2009-32, "Commercial Real Estate (CRE) Loans: Guidance on Prudent CRE Loan Workouts," which conveys interagency guidance on the topic, and the "Rating Credit Risk" booklet of the *Comptroller's Handbook.*

Loan Review

Periodic independent reviews should be conducted to verify the accuracy of ratings and the operational effectiveness of the bank's risk-rating processes. Objective reviews of credit risk levels and risk-management processes are essential to effective portfolio management. Loan review is a key internal control and an element of the safety and soundness standards that are described in the "Interagency Guidelines Establishing Standards For Safety And Soundness" found in appendix A of 12 CFR 30 (national banks) and 12 CFR 170 (federal savings associations). The "Loan Portfolio Management" booklet of the *Comptroller's Handbook* and attachment 1 of the "Interagency Policy Statement on the Allowance for Loan and Lease Losses" conveyed in OCC Bulletin 2006-47, "Allowance for Loan and Lease Losses (ALLL): Guidance and Frequently Asked Questions (FAQs) on the ALLL," provide additional guidance for the evaluation of a bank's loan review function.

Loan Workouts and Restructures

OCC Bulletin 2009-32, "Commercial Real Estate (CRE) Loans: Guidance on Prudent CRE Loan Workouts" conveys the interagency "Policy Statement on Prudent CRE Loan Workouts." Prudent loan workouts are often in the best interest of both banks and borrowers, particularly during difficult economic conditions. The guidance addresses supervisory expectations for risk management of loan workout programs, loan workout arrangements, classification of loans, and regulatory reporting and accounting considerations. Examples of loan workouts and their effect on loan classification and accounting treatment are provided in the guidance.

Risk Management Elements for Loan Workout Programs

A bank's management policies and practices for renewing and restructuring CRE loans should be appropriate for the complexity and nature of its lending activity and consistent with safe and sound lending practices and relevant regulatory reporting requirements. These practices should address

- management infrastructure to identify, control, and manage volume and complexity of the workout activity.
- documentation standards to verify the borrower's financial condition and collateral values.
- adequacy of MIS and internal controls to identify and track loan performance and risk, including concentration risk.
- management's responsibility to ensure that regulatory reports are consistent with regulatory reporting requirements (including GAAP) and supervisory guidance.
- effectiveness of loan collection procedures.
- adherence to statutory, regulatory and internal lending limits.
- collateral administration to ensure proper lien perfection of collateral interests for both real and personal property.
- an ongoing credit review function.

Banks that implement prudent loan workout arrangements will not be subject to examiner criticism for engaging in such efforts, even if the restructured loans have weaknesses that result in adverse credit classification, if management has

- a prudent workout policy.
- a well-conceived and prudent workout plan for an individual credit.
- an analysis of the borrower's global debt service.
- the ability to monitor the ongoing performance of the borrower and guarantor.
- an accurate and consistent internal loan grading system.
- an ALLL methodology that is consistent with GAAP and recognizes credit losses in a timely manner through provisions and charge-offs, as appropriate.

Key elements of a prudent workout plan include

- updated and comprehensive financial information on the borrower, real estate project, and any guarantor(s).
- current valuations of the collateral supporting the loan and the workout plan.
- analysis and determination of appropriate loan structure (e.g., term and amortization schedule), curtailment, covenants, or re-margining requirements.
- appropriate legal documentation for any changes to loan terms.

Loan workouts can take many forms, including a renewal or extension of loan terms, extension of additional credit, or a restructuring with or without concessions. A renewal or restructuring of a troubled credit should improve a bank's prospects for repayment of principal and interest. A bank should consider a borrower's repayment capacity, the support provided by guarantors, and the value of the collateral pledged on the debt.

Renewed or restructured loans to borrowers who have the ability to repay their debts under reasonable modified terms should not be subject to adverse classification solely because the value of the underlying collateral has declined to an amount that is less than the loan balance. Adverse classification of a restructured loan would be appropriate if, after the restructuring, well-defined weaknesses exist that jeopardize the orderly repayment of the loan in accordance with reasonable modified terms. The presence of a guarantee from a financially responsible guarantor may improve the prospects for repayment of the debt obligation and may be sufficient to preclude classification or reduce the severity of classification.

Accrual Status

For most loan types, banks may not accrue interest on any asset for which payment in full of principal or interest is not expected, or where principal or interest is 90 days or more delinquent unless the asset is both well secured and in the process of collection. The decision is based on repayment capacity and not tied directly to the value of underlying collateral.

For a restructured loan that is not already in nonaccrual status before the restructuring, the bank needs to consider whether the loan should be placed in nonaccrual status to ensure that income is not materially overstated. A loan that has been restructured so as to be reasonably assured of repayment of principal and interest and of performance according to prudent modified terms need not be maintained in nonaccrual status, provided the restructuring and any charge-off taken on the asset are supported by a current, well-documented credit evaluation of the borrower's financial condition and prospects for repayment under the revised terms. Otherwise, the restructured loan must remain in nonaccrual status.

In assessing accrual status, management should consider the borrower's sustained historical repayment performance for a reasonable period before the date on which the loan is returned to accrual status. A sustained period of repayment performance generally is a minimum of six months and would involve payments of cash or cash equivalents. In returning the asset to accrual status, sustained historical repayment performance for a reasonable time before the restructuring may be taken into account.

For more detailed criteria about placing a loan in nonaccrual status and returning a nonaccrual loan to accrual status, see the Federal Financial Institutions Examination Council's (FFIEC) call report instructions.

Troubled Debt Restructurings

All restructured loans should be evaluated to determine whether the loan should be reported as a troubled debt restructuring (TDR). For reporting purposes, a restructured loan is considered a TDR when the bank, for economic or legal reasons related to a borrower's financial difficulties, grants a concession to the borrower in modifying or renewing a loan that the bank would not otherwise consider. Guidance on reporting TDRs, including characteristics of modifications, is included in the FFIEC call report instructions and OCC Bulletin 2012-10, "Troubled Debt Restructurings: Supervisory Guidance on Accounting and Reporting Requirements."

Allowance for Loan and Lease Losses

For performing CRE loans, supervisory policies do not require automatic increases in the ALLL solely because the value of the collateral has declined to an amount less than the loan balance. Declines in collateral values should be considered, however, when calculating loss rates for affected groups of loans when estimating loan losses under the FASB ASC Subtopic 450-20, "Loss Contingencies." For more information, see OCC Bulletin 2006-47, "Allowance for Loan and Lease Losses (ALLL): Guidance and Frequently Asked Questions (FAQs) on the ALLL," and the OCC's *Bank Accounting Advisory Series*.

Foreclosure

Banks should have robust policies and procedures in place to address risks associated with foreclosed, or soon to be foreclosed, properties. Acquiring properties in satisfaction of debt (either for the bank or as servicer for another mortgagee) results in new or expanded risks, including operating risk and market valuation issues, compliance risk, and reputation risk. Banks should identify all risks and ensure they have policies and procedures for monitoring and controlling such risks.

The "Other Real Estate Owned" booklet of the *Comptroller's Handbook* discusses some of the risks presented by the foreclosure of commercial properties.

Examination Procedures

This booklet contains expanded procedures for examining specialized activities or specific products or services that warrant extra attention beyond the core assessment contained in the "Community Bank Supervision," "Large Bank Supervision," and "Federal Branches and Agencies Supervision" booklets of the *Comptroller's Handbook*. Examiners determine which expanded procedures to use, if any, during examination planning or after drawing preliminary conclusions during the core assessment.

Scope

These procedures are designed to help examiners tailor the examination to each bank and determine the scope of the CRE lending examination. This determination should consider work performed by internal and external auditors and other independent risk control functions and by other examiners on related examinations. Examiners need to perform only those objectives and steps that are relevant to the scope of the examination as determined by the following objective. Seldom will every objective or step of the expanded procedures be necessary.

Objective: Determine the scope of the CRE lending examination.

1. Review the examination scope memo and discuss examination goals and objectives with the examiner-in-charge (EIC) or loan portfolio manager (LPM) examiner.

2. Review the following for previously identified issues that require follow up. In consultation with the EIC, determine whether bank management has effectively responded to any adverse findings and implemented appropriate corrective actions.

   - Supervisory strategy.
   - Previous ROE and work papers, including the results of any previous CRE lending reviews.
   - Bank management's responses to previous examination findings.
   - Bank correspondence regarding CRE lending.
   - Audit reports and internal loan review reports and work papers, as necessary.

3. Obtain and review the Uniform Bank Performance Report (UBPR), Bank Expert Report (BERT), and other OCC reports—including any District Office analytical tools relating to CRE lending. Identify trends in growth rates, portfolio composition, concentrations, portfolio performance, pricing, and other factors that may affect the risk profile of the bank.

4. Obtain and review the bank's

    -   CRE lending policies and procedures, including those related to appraisals and environmental risk management.
    -   portfolio strategies, risk tolerance parameters, and risk management guidelines.
    -   loan commitment report showing commitments and undisbursed funds.
    -   internal loan review reports.
    -   loan trial balance, past due accounts, and loans in nonaccrual status.
    -   credit risk rating reports, including a list of "watch" credits.
    -   problem loan reports for adversely rated CRE and construction loans.
    -   concentration reports and board approved concentration limits.
    -   exception reports.
    -   financial statement tracking reports.
    -   real estate tax monitoring reports.
    -   board or loan committee reports and minutes related to CRE lending activities.
    -   loans for which terms have been modified by a reduction of the interest rate or principal payment, by a deferral of interest or principal, or by other restructuring of payment terms.
    -   loans on which interest has been capitalized subsequent to initial underwriting.
    -   over-disbursed loans.
    -   loan participations purchased and sold since the previous examination.
    -   shared national credits, if applicable.
    -   information regarding the composition of the credit department including the organizational chart, resumes of senior staff, and lending authorities.
    -   loans to insiders of the bank or any affiliate of the bank.

5. Discuss the bank's CRE lending activities with management. Discussions should address

    -   management's strategy for the CRE lending function, including
        -   growth goals.
        -   existing and potential sources of loan demand.
        -   new loan types, property types, or geographic regions.
        -   new marketing strategies and initiatives.
    -   the staff's experience and ability to implement strategic initiatives and achieve strategic goals.
    -   current and projected concentrations of credit, as well as management's plans to manage concentrations.
    -   significant changes in policies, procedures, underwriting, personnel, and control systems.
    -   internal or external factors that could affect the portfolio.
    -   stress testing practices.
    -   observations from examiner review of internal bank reports, as well as OCC and other third-party generated reports.

- the extent of syndicated distribution and participation activities as a buyer and a seller, if applicable.

6. Based on analysis of the information received and discussions with bank management, determine the factors behind changes in loan growth, loan portfolio composition, customer or product types, underwriting criteria, or market focus. Consider

   - growth and acquisitions.
   - board or management changes.
   - changes in risk tolerance limits including concentrations.
   - changes in external factors, such as
     - national, regional, and local economies.
     - real estate markets.
     - industry outlook.
     - regulatory framework.
     - technological changes.

7. As examination procedures are performed, test for compliance with applicable laws, rules, regulations, and established policies. Confirm the existence of appropriate internal controls. Identify any areas that have inadequate supervision or pose undue risk. Discuss with the EIC the need to perform additional procedures.

8. Based on findings resulting from the previous steps and in consultation with the EIC and other appropriate supervisors, determine the examination's scope and volume of testing necessary to meet supervisory objectives. Select from the following expanded procedures, internal control questions, and verification procedures necessary to meet the examination objectives.

Quantity of Risk

Conclusion: The quantity of each associated risk is (low, moderate, or high).

Determine the quantity of risk associated with CRE lending activities. Consider the "Quantity of Credit Risk Indicators" in appendix A of this booklet, as appropriate.

Credit Risk

Objective: To determine the quantity of credit risk associated with CRE lending.

1. Analyze the quantity of credit risk. The analysis should consider such factors as the products, markets, geographies, technologies, volumes, size of the exposures, quality metrics, and concentrations. Consider whether the "Portfolio Stress Test Tool for Income Producing Commercial Real Estate" should be used by the examiner to analyze the quantity of risk posed by concentrations.

2. Assess the effect of external factors, including economic, industry, competitive, and market conditions.

3. Assess the effect of potential legislative, regulatory, accounting, and technological changes.

4. Obtain the loan trial balance and select a sample of loans to be reviewed. Selection of the sample should be consistent with the examination objectives, supervisory strategy, and district business plans. Refer to the "Sampling Methodologies" booklet of the *Comptroller's Handbook* for guidance. Consider

   - new, large loans.
   - new loan types.
   - loans originated in new geographic regions.
   - loans at or above the legal lending limit.
   - loans to insiders of the bank or any affiliates.
   - over-disbursed loans.
   - loans with multiple renewals or extensions, particularly construction loans.
   - special mention loans or classified loans.
   - loans with significant policy or underwriting exceptions.
   - loans with modified repayment terms.

5. Obtain and review credit files for all borrowers in the sample and prepare line sheets for the sampled credits. Line sheets should contain sufficient analysis to determine the credit rating; support any criticisms of underwriting, servicing, or credit administration practices; and document any violations of law. In particular, file readers should:

A. Determine the primary source of repayment of each loan and evaluate its adequacy.

- For income-producing properties, assess the adequacy of cash flow to meet debt service requirements. Comment as necessary on trends in NOI, vacancy, and expenses. Review current rent rolls and leases, and assess the quality and mix of tenants. Note any significant volume of leases scheduled to expire. Analyze the potential effect on future debt-service coverage from tenant turnover.
- For owner-occupied buildings, concentrate analysis on the ability of the owner's cash flow to service debt.
- For construction loans,
  - determine whether project feasibility supported the bank's decision to extend credit.
  - evaluate the construction budget and determine if cost estimates appear reliable.
  - assess the project's status to determine whether it is progressing according to plan.
  - determine whether material changes have been made to the plans and whether these changes are reflected in the construction budget.
  - determine whether material changes have been made to the construction budget and the reasons for these changes.
  - determine whether sufficient funds remain available in each category of the construction budget to complete the project.
  - assess adequacy of the interest reserve in light of construction progress.
  - review adequacy of reports used to monitor construction progress, advances, sales, leasing, etc. Ascertain if inspection reports support disbursements to date and are performed by an independent party.
  - determine the source of permanent financing. If different from the current lender, determine whether take-out arrangements have been secured and assess compliance with take-out covenants.

B. Evaluate external factors, such as economic conditions, and the effect on supply and demand, rental rates, vacancy rates, interest rates, capitalization rates, and NOI.

C. Analyze secondary sources of repayment provided by guarantors, financial sponsors, or endorsers. If the financial condition of the borrower warrants concern, determine the guarantor's, sponsor's, or endorser's capacity and willingness to repay the credit.

D. Evaluate sufficiency of collateral coverage. Determine whether the appraisals or evaluations were obtained consistent with regulatory requirements (12 CFR 34, subpart C for national banks and 12 CFR 164 for federal savings associations) and meet USPAP. File reviewers should consider

- timing of the appraisal and loan origination date.
- whether the appraisal was commissioned independent of the lending function.
- appraiser qualifications specific to the type of real estate.

- appropriateness of the valuation method used and the definition of value provided.
- reasonableness and documentation of assumptions used to derive the collateral value.
- quality and timing of appraisal review.
- whether new appraisals or evaluations were obtained when conditions warranted.
- whether LTV ratios are accurately calculated, and whether LTV exceptions are appropriately documented and approved.

E. Determine whether the borrower is in compliance with the loan agreement and financial covenants.

F. Document all significant loan policy and underwriting exceptions and whether exceptions were appropriately approved.

G. Assign risk ratings to the sampled credits. Refer to risk rating guidance in this booklet, OCC Bulletin 2009-32, "Commercial Real Estate (CRE) Loans: Guidance on Prudent CRE Loan Workouts," and the "Rating Credit Risk" booklet of the *Comptroller's Handbook*.

6. Review completed line sheets and summarize loan sample results. The examiner responsible for the CRE lending review should

- identify recommended loan risk-rating downgrades and ensure such decisions are appropriately documented.
- maintain a list of structurally weak loans reviewed.
- maintain a list of loans for which examiners were unable to determine the risk rating because of lack of information.
- maintain a list of loans not supported by current and complete financial information and loans in which collateral documentation is deficient.
- summarize whether policy, underwriting, or documentation exceptions were appropriately identified and approved. If exceptions are not being accurately identified and reported, including SLTV exceptions, determine the cause and discuss with management.

7. If the bank actively engages in loan participation purchases and sales,

- test participation agreements to determine that the parties share in the risks and contractual payments on a pro rata basis.
- determine whether the books and records properly reflect the bank's asset or liability.
- determine whether the bank exercises similar controls over loans serviced for others as for its own loans.
- investigate any loans or participations sold immediately before the examination to determine whether any were sold to avoid criticism during the examination.

8. If the bank actively engages in the Interagency Shared National Credit (SNC) program,

   • determine whether qualifying credits were sampled as part of the SNC review process. For each loan in the sample that is also a SNC, transcribe appropriate information to the line sheets. Grade the loan the same as was done at the SNC review. Do not perform additional file work on SNC loans.
   • determine that the bank, as lead or agent in a credit, exercises similar controls and procedures over syndications and participations sold as it exercises for loans in its own portfolio.
   • determine that the bank, as a participant in a credit agented by another party, exercises similar controls over those participations purchased as it exercises for loans it has generated directly.

9. If the bank actively engages in FHA-insured loans,

   • determine that a valid certificate of insurance or guaranty is on file by reviewing management's procedures to obtain such insurance or guaranty or by testing a representative sample of such loans.
   • determine that required delinquency reports are being submitted.

10. Discuss the results of the loan sample with the EIC or LPM examiner and bank management.

Associated Risks

In addition to credit risk, CRE lending can generate interest rate risk, liquidity risk, operational risk, compliance risk, strategic risk, and reputation risk. These risks and how CRE lending can expose the bank to these risks are discussed in the "Introduction" section of this booklet.

Objective: To determine the quantity of other risks associated with CRE lending activities.

1. Assess the effect of CRE lending on the quantity of interest rate risk. Consider

   • the effect of interest rate changes on both the borrowers and the bank.
   • underwriting terms such as tenor and management's pricing structure, e.g., fixed vs. variable interest rates and the potential exposure to different pricing indices.
   • off-balance-sheet exposures.
   • the quality and results of sensitivity analysis and portfolio stress testing.

2. Assess the effect of CRE lending on the quantity of liquidity risk. Consider

   • CRE and construction portfolio growth rates and the corresponding funding strategies.

- the composition of the CRE portfolio and the ability to convert the loans to cash. Consider the level of properties under construction or completed properties that have not reached stabilization as these properties are less liquid.
- current market conditions.

3. Assess the effect of CRE lending on the quantity of operational risk. Consider

- any operational losses resulting from the CRE lending function.
- control weaknesses identified by audit, loan review, or any other control group.
- the quality of board oversight.
- the quality of credit administration, e.g., segregation of duties, financial analysis, construction controls, and documentation standards.
- the quality and independence of the audit and loan review functions.
- staffing turnover affecting the CRE function.
- responses to the Internal Control Questionnaire.

4. Assess the effect of CRE lending on the quantity of compliance risk. Consider

- the bank's history of compliance with lending related laws and regulations, particularly those established regarding appraisals, insider lending activities, legal lending limits, and affiliates, as well as safe and sound banking practices.
- for federal savings associations, if the association is approaching or has exceeded its HOLA investment limit of 400 percent of total capital for nonresidential real estate loans (12 USC 1464(c)).
- the quality of the bank's environmental risk management program and losses attributed to liabilities resulting from environmental risk.
- the quality of the controls over CRE lending activities.
- compliance with internal policies and procedures.

5. Assess the effect of CRE lending on the level of strategic risk. Consider

- management's strategy regarding CRE lending and the potential effect on risk including those posed by concentrations.
- board oversight of strategic initiatives.
- the adequacy of the bank's program for monitoring economic and market conditions.
- the ability of the staff to implement CRE strategies without exposing the bank to unwarranted risk.
- the adequacy of CRE risk-management systems.

6. Assess the effect of CRE lending on the level of reputation risk. Consider

- the bank's effectiveness in meeting the CRE and construction credit needs of the communities it serves.
- the volume of foreclosures and the nature of foreclosure practices.
- the volume of litigation related to CRE lending activities.

Quality of Risk Management

Conclusion: The quality of risk management is (strong, satisfactory, or weak).

Determine the quality of risk management considering all risks associated with CRE lending. Consider the "Quality of Credit Risk Management Indicators" in appendix B of this booklet, as appropriate.

Policies

Policies are statements of actions adopted by a bank to pursue certain objectives. Policies often set standards (on risk tolerances, for example) and should be consistent with the bank's underlying mission, values, and principles. A policy review should always be triggered when the bank's objectives or standards change.

Objective: To determine whether the board has adopted effective policies that are consistent with safe and sound banking practices and appropriate to the size, nature, and scope of the bank's CRE lending activities.

1. Evaluate relevant policies to determine whether they provide appropriate guidance for managing the bank's CRE lending activities, reflecting consideration of the "Interagency Guidelines for Real Estate Lending Policies" as found in subpart D of 12 CFR 34 (national banks) and 12 CFR 160.101 (federal savings associations), the bank's size and nature and scope of its operations, and the level of risk that is acceptable to its board of directors. Do the bank's policies

    *   establish prudent underwriting standards, including LTV limits that are clear and measurable?
    *   establish loan administration procedures for the real estate portfolio?
    *   establish documentation, approval, and reporting requirements to monitor compliance with the bank's real estate lending policy?
    *   require the monitoring of conditions in the bank's real estate lending market to ensure that its lending policies continue to be appropriate for current market conditions?

    Consider

    *   the size, risk profile, and financial condition of the bank.
    *   significant CRE concentrations.
    *   current and projected market conditions.
    *   credit administration policies.
    *   construction risk-management policies.
    *   environmental risk-management policies.
    *   loan documentation standards.

- the loan workout function.
- compliance with the real estate lending standards outlined in 12 CFR 34, subpart D (national banks) and 12 CFR 160.101 (federal savings associations).

2. Evaluate the bank's appraisal and evaluation policies and their compliance with 12 CFR 34, subpart C (national banks) and 12 CFR 164 (federal savings associations) and OCC Bulletin 2010-42, "Sound Practices for Appraisals and Evaluations: Interagency Appraisal and Evaluation Guidelines." Determine whether policies

- provide for the independence of the persons ordering, performing, and reviewing appraisals or evaluations.
- establish selection criteria and procedures for engaging appraisers and persons who perform evaluations.
- establish criteria and procedures to evaluate and monitor the ongoing performance of appraisers and persons who perform evaluations.
- ensure that appraisals comply with the agencies' appraisal regulations and are consistent with supervisory guidance.
- ensure that appraisals and evaluations contain sufficient information and analysis to support the credit decision.
- maintain criteria for the content and appropriate use of evaluations consistent with safe and sound banking practices.
- provide for the receipt of the appraisal or evaluation report in a timely manner to facilitate the credit decision.
- provide for the review of the appraisal or evaluation report and the documentation of the review in a timely manner to facilitate the credit decision.
- develop criteria to assess whether an existing appraisal or evaluation may be used to support a subsequent transaction.
- implement internal controls that promote compliance with these program standards, including those related to monitoring third-party arrangements.
- establish criteria for monitoring collateral values.
- establish criteria for assessing and documenting whether an existing appraisal or evaluation, when relied upon, remains valid.
- establish criteria for obtaining appraisals or evaluations for transactions that are not otherwise covered by the appraisal requirements of the agencies' appraisal regulations.

3. Determine whether policies establish risk limits or positions and delineate prudent actions to be taken if limits are exceeded. If the bank maintains CRE concentrations, evaluate compliance with OCC Bulletin 2006-46, "Concentrations in Commercial Real Estate Lending, Sound Risk Management Practices: Interagency Guidance on CRE Concentration Risk Management." In particular, assess the effectiveness of

- CRE concentration assessments.
- board oversight.
- MIS.

- market analysis.
- credit underwriting standards.
- portfolio stress testing and sensitivity analysis.
- the credit risk review function.

4. Verify that the board of directors periodically reviews and approves the bank's CRE lending policies.

Processes

Processes are the procedures, programs, and practices that impose order on a bank's pursuit of its objectives. Processes define how daily activities are carried out. Effective processes are consistent with the underlying policies and are governed by appropriate checks and balances (such as internal controls).

Objective: To determine whether the bank has processes in place to define how CRE lending activities are carried out.

1. Evaluate whether processes are effective, consistent with underlying policies, and effectively communicated to appropriate staff. Consider

   - whether the board of directors has clearly communicated objectives and risk limits for the CRE loan portfolio to management and staff.
   - whether communication to key personnel within the CRE function is timely.

2. Determine whether appropriate internal controls are in place and functioning as designed. Complete the Internal Control Questionnaire in this booklet, if necessary, to make this determination. Consider

   - nature and scope of the bank's real estate lending activities.
   - size and financial condition of the bank.
   - quality of management and internal controls.
   - expertise and size of the lending and loan administration staff.
   - market conditions.

3. Determine the quality of credit administration. Consider observations from the loan sample, including

   - the volume, trend, and nature of loan policy and underwriting exceptions.
   - the soundness of underwriting and adherence to standards and policies.
   - the timeliness of financial statements and their analysis.
   - loan covenant monitoring and enforcement.
   - Risk-rating changes.
   - construction loan administration including draw and disbursement practices.
   - loan review or audit findings pertaining to loan administration.

4. Evaluate the bank's appraisal and evaluation program. Consider the quality, timing, and independence of the appraisal and appraisal review functions, and management's criteria for obtaining, updating or determining the validity of appraisals or evaluations when appropriate. Do the bank's processes ensure that

   - persons selected possess the requisite education, expertise, and experience to competently complete the assignment?
   - persons selected to perform appraisals hold the appropriate state certification or license at the time of the assignment?
   - appraisal reports and evaluations are reviewed and the review is documented?
   - persons selected are independent and have no direct, indirect, or prospective interest, financial or otherwise, in the property or the transaction and capable of rendering an unbiased opinion?
   - methods, assumptions, and value conclusions are reasonable and contain sufficient information and analysis on which to base sound credit decisions?
   - appraisals or evaluations comply with the agencies' appraisal regulations and supervisory guidelines as well as the bank's policies?

Personnel

Personnel are the bank staff and managers who execute or oversee processes. Personnel should be qualified and competent, and should perform appropriately. They should understand the bank's mission, values, principles, policies, and processes. Banks should design compensation programs to attract, develop, and retain qualified personnel. In addition, compensation programs should be structured in a manner that encourages strong risk-management practices.

Objective: To determine management's ability to supervise CRE lending in a safe and sound manner.

1. Given the scope and complexity of the bank's CRE activities, assess the management structure and staffing. Consider

   - the level of staffing.
   - the staff's ability to support current operations and planned growth.
   - whether reporting lines encourage open communication and limit the chances of conflicts of interest.
   - the level of staff turnover.
   - the use of outsourcing arrangements.
   - capability to address identified deficiencies.
   - responsiveness to regulatory, accounting, industry, and technological changes.

2. Given the scope and complexity of the bank's CRE activities, assess the experience, education and training, and demonstrated expertise and competency of management and staff. Consider

- the suitability of the incumbent's experience and training for his/her position.
- the availability, adequacy, and requirements for training to keep management and staff current with regulatory and other changes affecting the bank.
- the experience and training or education of individuals responsible for the bank's appraisal and evaluation program including licensing or certification for any staff appraisers.

3. Assess performance management and compensation programs. Consider whether these programs measure and reward performance that aligns with the bank's strategic objectives and risk tolerance.

   If the bank offers incentive compensation programs, ensure that the programs are consistent with OCC Bulletin 2010-24, "Incentive Compensation: Interagency Guidance on Sound Incentive Compensation Policies," including compliance with three key principles: (1) provide employees with incentives that appropriately balance risk and reward; (2) be compatible with effective controls and risk management; and (3) be supported by strong corporate governance, including active and effective oversight by the bank's board of directors.

Control Systems

Control systems are the functions (such as internal and external audits, risk review, and quality assurance) and information systems that bank managers use to measure performance, make decisions about risk, and assess the effectiveness of processes. Control functions should have clear reporting lines, adequate resources, and appropriate authority. MISs should provide timely, accurate, and relevant feedback.

Objective: To determine whether the bank has systems in place to provide accurate and timely assessments of the risks associated with its CRE lending function.

1. Evaluate the effectiveness of monitoring systems to identify, measure, and track concentrations and exceptions to policies and established limits.

2. Determine whether MIS provides timely, accurate, and useful information to evaluate growth, asset quality, concentrations, performance and other trends, and risk levels in the bank's CRE lending activities.

3. Assess the scope, frequency, effectiveness, and independence of the internal and external audits of the CRE lending function. Consider the qualifications of audit personnel and evaluate accessibility to necessary information and the board of directors.

4. Assess the effectiveness of loan review. Evaluate the scope, frequency, effectiveness, and independence of loan review, as well as their ability to identify and report emerging problems. Determine whether loan review reports address the

- classification of loans.
- identification and measurement of impairments.
- loan documentation.
- quality of the CRE portfolio.
- trend in portfolio quality.
- quality of significant relationships.
- level and trend of policy, underwriting, and pricing exceptions.

5. Assess the effectiveness of the bank's systems that ensure the quality and independence of appraisals and evaluations. Consider

- whether reporting lines are independent of loan production and collection.
- the effectiveness of review procedures.
- the effectiveness of the appraiser engagement process.

Conclusions

Conclusion: The aggregate level of each associated risk is (low, moderate, or high). The direction of each associated risk is (increasing, stable, or decreasing).

Objective: To determine, document, and communicate overall findings and conclusions regarding the examination of the bank's CRE lending activities.

1. Discuss preliminary examination findings and conclusions with the EIC, including

   - effect on the core assessment of asset quality and management.
   - quantity of associated risks (as noted in this booklet's "Introduction" section).
   - quality of risk management.
   - aggregate level and direction of associated risks.
   - overall risk in CRE lending activities.
   - violations and other concerns.

2. If substantive safety and soundness concerns remain unresolved that may have a material, adverse effect on the bank, further expand the scope of the examination by completing verification procedures.

3. Discuss examination findings with bank management, including violations, recommendations, and conclusions about risks and risk management practices. If necessary, obtain commitments for corrective action.

4. Complete the following table summarizing credit and other risks (interest rate, liquidity, operational, compliance, strategic, and reputation) in the bank's CRE lending activities

Summary of Risks Associated With CRE Lending				
Risk category	Quantity of risk (Low, moderate, high)	Quality of risk management (Weak, satisfactory, strong)	Aggregate level of risk (Low, moderate, high)	Direction of risk (Increasing, stable, decreasing)
Credit				
Interest rate				
Liquidity				
Operational				
Compliance				
Strategic				
Reputation				

5. Compose conclusion comments, highlighting any issues that should be included in the ROE. Include conclusions for

- the portfolio's asset quality.
- adequacy of policies and procedures and reasonableness of underwriting standards.
- volume, trend, and severity of underwriting and policy exceptions.
- CRE concentrations and compliance with interagency guidance.
- loan sample results including risk-rating changes, compliance with loan policy, and quality of underwriting.
- quality of board oversight and portfolio supervision.
- appropriateness and attainability of strategic goals.
- quality of staffing.
- accuracy and timeliness of MIS.
- effectiveness of credit administration and internal controls.
- effectiveness of the bank's appraisal and evaluation program.
- reliability of internal risk ratings.
- the extent to which CRE lending activities and risk-management practices affect interrelated risks including interest rate risk, liquidity risk, operational risk, compliance risk, strategic risk, and reputation risk.
- compliance with applicable laws, rules, and regulations.
- recommended corrective actions and management's commitment to implement, if necessary.

6. If necessary, compose a Matters Requiring Attention (MRA) comment.

7. Update the OCC's information system and any applicable ROE schedules or tables.

8. Write a memorandum specifically setting out what the OCC should do in the future to effectively supervise CRE lending activities in the bank, including time periods, staffing, and workdays required.

9. Update, organize, and reference work papers in accordance with OCC policy.

10. Ensure any paper or electronic media that contain sensitive bank or customer information are appropriately disposed of or secured.

Internal Control Questionnaire

An internal control questionnaire (ICQ) helps the examiner assess a bank's internal controls for an area. ICQs typically address standard controls that provide day-to-day protection of bank assets and financial records. The examiner decides the extent to which it is necessary to complete or update ICQs during examination planning or after reviewing the findings and conclusions of the core assessment.

Policies

1. Has the board of directors, consistent with its duties and responsibilities, adopted real estate loan policies consistent with safe and sound banking practices and appropriate to the size of the bank and to the nature and scope of its operations? In particular, do the bank's policies

   - identify the geographic areas in which the bank considers lending?
   - establish a loan portfolio diversification policy and set limits for real estate loans by type and geographic market (e.g., limits on construction and other types of higher risk loans)?
   - establish policies for the identification, monitoring, and management of concentrations?
   - identify appropriate terms and conditions by type of real estate loan?
   - establish loan origination and approval procedures, both generally and by size and type of loan?
   - establish prudent underwriting standards that are clear and measurable, including
     - maximum loan amount by type of property?
     - maximum loan maturities by type of property?
     - amortization schedules?
     - pricing structure for different types of real estate loans?
     - LTV limits no greater than specified in the "Interagency Guidelines for Real Estate Lending Policies" found in subpart D of 12 CFR 34 (national banks) and 12 CFR 160.101 (federal savings associations)?

2. For development and construction projects, and completed commercial properties, do the bank's underwriting standards also establish

   - requirements for feasibility studies and sensitivity and risk analyses (e.g., sensitivity of income projections to changes in economic variables such as interest rates, vacancy rates, or operating expenses)?
   - minimum requirements for initial investment and maintenance of hard equity by the borrower (e.g., cash or unencumbered investment in the underlying property)?
   - minimum standards for net worth, cash flow, and debt-service coverage of the borrower or underlying property?
   - standards for the acceptability of and limits on nonamortizing loans?

- standards for the acceptability of and limits on the financing of the borrower's soft costs on a project?
- standards for the acceptability of and limits on the use of interest reserves?
- preleasing and presale requirements for income-producing property?
- presale and minimum unit release requirements for ADC loans?
- limits on partial recourse or nonrecourse loans and requirements for guarantor support?
- requirements for loan agreements for construction loans?
- requirements for take-out commitments, if applicable?
- minimum covenants for loan agreements?

3. Has the bank established loan administration policies for its real estate portfolio that address

- documentation, including:
  - type and frequency of financial statements, including requirements for verification of information provided by the borrower?
  - type and frequency of collateral appraisals and evaluations?
- loan closing and disbursement procedures, including the supervised disbursement of proceeds on construction loans?
- payment processing?
- escrow administration?
- collateral administration, including inspection procedures for construction loans?
- loan payoffs?
- collection and foreclosure, including
  - delinquency and follow-up procedures?
  - foreclosure timing?
  - extensions and other forms of forbearance?
  - acceptance of deeds in lieu of foreclosure?
- claims processing (e.g., seeking recovery on a defaulted loan covered by a government guaranty or insurance program)?
- servicing and participation agreements?

4. Are procedures in effect to monitor compliance with the bank's real estate lending policies?

- Are exception loans of a significant size reported individually to the board of directors?
- Are the numbers and types of exceptions monitored so that the loan policy and lending practices can be periodically evaluated?
- Are loans in excess of the SLTV limits identified in the bank's records and their aggregate amount reported at least quarterly to the board of directors?
- Are concentrations monitored and measured against established limits?

5. Does the bank monitor conditions in the real estate market in its lending area to ensure that its real estate lending policies continue to be appropriate, given market conditions?

6. Are the bank's real estate lending policies reviewed and approved by the board of directors at least annually?

Appraisal and Evaluation Program

7. Are the bank's policy or procedures for appraisals and evaluations approved by the board of directors at least annually?

8. Are the bank's policy and procedures for appraisals and evaluations in writing and readily available to bank personnel?

9. If the bank has an appraisal department, is it independent and isolated from influence by loan production and collection staff?

10. Does the bank have separate policies and procedures for each department or line of business?

11. If the bank maintains a list of approved appraisers,

    - does the bank investigate the qualifications of appraisers before placing them on the list of approved appraisers?
    - does the bank periodically test appraisals to ensure that inadequate appraisers are not being used and are removed from the approved list if one is used?
    - does the bank have procedures in place for the removal and reinstatement of appraisers from the approved list if one is used?

12. Does the bank have an internal review procedure to determine whether appraisal policies and procedures are being followed consistently?

13. Does appraisal policy address when appraisals are required?

14. Does appraisal policy address when appraisals are not required, but evaluations are?

15. Does appraisal policy address when neither appraisals nor evaluations are needed?

16. Does the bank's policy or procedures provide for the monitoring of real estate collateral values for other real estate owned (OREO)?

17. Does the bank's policy or procedures provide for the monitoring of real estate collateral values for troubled real estate loans (special mention or substandard)?

18. Does the bank's policy or procedures provide for the monitoring of real estate collateral values for portfolio loans?

Appraisals—External

19. Are appraisals ordered by the appraisal department or an entitiy or employee that is independent of loan production and collection functions?

20. Are appraisers selected and engaged for each assignment based on their competency and experience in appraising similar properties in the subject property's market?

21. Does the bank make it clear that loan officers cannot recommend an appraiser to be considered for or excluded from an assignment?

22. Are there procedures for appraisal ordering?

23. Does the bank provide written instructions or engagement letters to the engaged appraiser?

24. Is the appraiser instructed to develop an opinion of market value as defined in the appraisal regulation?

25. Is the appraiser isolated from influence, pressure, or coercion?

26. Does the bank ensure that appraisers are paid a customary and reasonable fee?

Appraisals—Internal

27. Are staff appraisers appropriately licensed or certified and competent for the assignment?

28. Does the bank occasionally have appraisals performed by staff reviewed by external appraisers?

Appraisal Review Function

29. Does the bank's policy require that every CRE appraisal be reviewed and is the policy followed?

30. Does the bank have procedures to evaluate and address the competence of reviewers?

31. Are appraisals reviewed and approved before funds are advanced?

32. Are any appraisal reviews outsourced? If so,

- does bank policy state when such outsourcing is to occur?
- are procedures in place to test the quality of outsourced reviews?
- does the reviewer utilize bank developed review documentation and specifications?
- does the bank have a quality control procedure in place for these reviews?

33. For internally performed reviews, is the employee independent of the loan production and collection functions?

34. Are all appraisals reviewed and is each review documented?

Evaluations

35. Has the bank developed appropriate procedures for when and how evaluations may be performed?

36. Has the bank developed procedures to evaluate the experience and competency of evaluators?

37. Do bank employees outside the appraisal department prepare evaluations? Is their independence ensured by precluding them from the loan production and collection functions?

38. Is there a list of approved internal evaluators?

39. Is there training for internal evaluators?

40. Is there a standard evaluation form?

41. Are evaluations prepared in compliance with the requirements of OCC Bulletin 2010-42, "Sound Practices for Appraisals and Evaluations: Interagency Appraisal and Evaluation Guidelines"?

42. Are procedures in place to review evaluations before funds are advanced?

43. Are all evaluations reviewed and is each review documented?

Appraisal Reviews

Reviews should consider the following.

44. Is it clear that the appraiser was independently engaged? Is the engagement letter included and, if so, does the letter indicate that the bank or another financial services institution engaged the appraiser?

45. Are the report and certification signed by an appraiser possessing appropriate credentials and sufficient experience for the given real estate related financial transaction? Is the appraiser an appropriate choice for the appraisal assignment? If a fee appraiser was engaged directly by the bank, has the bank performed appropriate due diligence on the appraiser?

46. Are the bank's instructions to the appraiser (generally in the form of an engagement letter) included? Is the appraiser's scope of work sufficient to develop a credible estimate of value? Does the appraisal support the bank's lending decision?

47. Is the appropriate ownership interest appraised, and are any assumptions and limiting conditions consistent with the bank's intended collateral position in the transaction?

48. Is the "as-is" market value reported?

49. Are there any significant internal or external factors to the property that may affect the future cash flow or value of the property? For example,

   - does the report address whether the site and improvements are suitable for the market and can the property sustain its historical cash flow?
   - based on the information in the report, can the reviewer determine the subject's relative position within its submarket and among its competing properties?
   - does the report address future supply and demand? How might that affect the subject property?
   - does the appraisal of the property anticipate the need for, and expense involved with, any replacements or improvements?

50. Is the property description complete, and does it include

   - the actual or approximate year built or anticipated date of completion?
   - property condition analysis?
   - building areas and dimensions with reference to the source of these?
   - adequate photos of improvements?
   - overall evaluation of construction quality, design, layout, and appearance?

51. If applicable, does the history of the property include

   - previous three years of sales?
   - analysis of previous sales?
   - analysis of current agreement of sale?
   - current option or listing?
   - changes to the property?

52. If the property is income-producing, are the historical operating statements analyzed, and are the property's projected income and expenses supportable, given the market? For example, does the report consider

   - strength of the tenants?
   - tenant rollover and anticipated rents?
   - probability of lease renewals?
   - terms of outstanding leases and NOI compared with budgets?

- current and projected vacancy and absorption rates?
- effective rental rates or sales prices including any concessions?
- marketing and other re-leasing costs?
- property's age?
- expertise of property management?
- effect of any planned or new construction or renovation coming on line in the market area?
- analysis of discount and capitalization rates?

53. For an appraisal report that elicits a value of the enterprise, such as "going-concern value," does it allocate that value among the three components of the total value: (1) the market value of the real estate, (2) the personal property value, and (3) the value of intangibles? (the bank may rely only on the opinion of the real estate's market value in going-concern appraisals to support the federally related transaction.)

54. If the sales comparison approach is the primary approach to value, are the comparables truly comparable with respect to property characteristics and location, and does the appraiser clearly discuss and support the adjustments?

55. Are the assumptions logical and supportable with market data?

56. If significant differences are cited from past performance for underwriting criteria such as lease rates, expenses and absorption, is there adequate explanation?

57. Are the determinants of the value conclusion reasonable? For example,

- are units of comparison (such as market prices per square foot or price per unit) consistent with those cited in comparables?
- is the capitalization or discount rate supportable, and does it appear reasonable in terms of the class, property type, and market conditions?
- does the cost exceed or closely approximate value? If the project is not economically feasible, what is the borrower's and banks' motivation to engage in the transaction?

Other

58. Does the bank require that documentation files (e.g., credit or collateral files) include appraisal reports?

59. Does the bank require that documentation files (e.g., credit or collateral files) include appraisal reviews?

60. Does bank policy note that residential (one- to four-unit) appraisals must be provided to borrowers upon request (Regulation B)?

61. Are appraisal fees paid directly by the bank?

62. Are appraisal fees the same amount regardless of whether the loan is granted?

Construction Loan Applications

Questions 63 through 100 focus on real estate construction lending. Additional questions concerning other applicable internal controls for real estate lending resume with question 101.

63. Does the bank require

- detailed resumes of the contractor's and major subcontractors' construction experience, as well as other projects under construction?
- current and historical financial statements?
- trade reputation checks?
- credit checks?
- bonding company checks?

64. Do project cost estimates include

- land and construction costs?
- off-site improvement expenses?
- cost of legal services?
- loan interest, supervisory fees, and insurance expenses?

65. Does the bank require a line-item budget or cost breakdown for each construction stage?

66. Does the bank require that cost estimates of more complicated projects be reviewed by qualified personnel, e.g., architect, construction engineer, or independent estimator?

67. Do cost budgets include the amount and source of the builder's or owner's equity contribution?

Loan Agreements and Other Documents

68. Are the loan agreement and other documents reviewed by counsel and other experts to determine that improvement specifications conform to

- building codes?
- subdivision regulations?
- zoning and ordinances?
- title or ground lease restrictions?
- health regulations?
- known or projected environmental protection considerations?
- specifications required under the National Flood Insurance Program?
- provisions in tenant leases?

- specifications approved by the permanent financier when applicable?
- specifications required by the completion bonding company or guarantors?

69. Does the bank require all change orders to be approved in writing by

- the bank?
- permanent financier if permanent funding not provided by the bank?
- architect or supervising engineer?
- prime tenants bound by firm leases or letters of intent to lease?
- completion bonding company?

70. Does the loan agreement establish a date for project completion?

71. Does the loan agreement require that

- on-site inspections be permitted?
- disbursement of funds be made as work progresses?
- the bank be allowed to withhold disbursements if work is not performed in accordance with approved specifications?
- a portion of the loan proceeds be retained pending satisfactory completion of the construction?
- the lender be allowed to assume prompt and complete control of the project in the event of default and an assignment of all development and construction-related contracts and agreements?
- the contractor carry builder's risk and workmen's compensation insurance?
- builder's risk insurance be on a nonreporting form or a reporting form that requires periodic increases in the project's value to be reported to the insurance company?
- the bank authorize individual tract housing starts?
- periodic sales reports be submitted from tract developers?
- periodic reports on tract houses occupied under rental or lease purchase option agreements be submitted?
- periodic reports be submitted on the status of any other projects in which the developer may be involved in?

Collateral

72. Does the bank place primary collateral reliance on first liens on real estate?

73. Does the bank temper the collateral reliance placed on

- ground leases?
- conditional sales contracts?

74. Does the bank require that construction loans

- be limited to a percent of the completed cost or market value of the project?
- be subject to the bank's own take-out commitment be limited to a percent of the appraised value of the completed project?
- be limited to the floor of a take-out commitment predicated on achievement of rents or lease occupancy?

75. Do construction loan policies preclude the issuance of standby commitments to "gap finance" projects with take-out conditions regarding rentals or occupancy?

76. Are unsecured credit lines to contractors or developers who are also being financed by secured construction loans supervised by

- the construction loan department?
- the officer supervising the construction loan?

Inspections

77. Are inspection requirements noted in

- the loan agreement?
- take-out commitment and tri-party buy and sell agreement, if applicable?

78. Are inspections conducted on an irregular schedule?

79. Are inspection reports sufficiently detailed to support disbursements?

80. Are inspectors independent and competent?

81. Are inspectors rotated?

82. Are spot checks made of the inspectors' work?

83. Do inspectors determine compliance with plans and specifications as well as progress of work?

Disbursements

84. Are disbursements

- advanced on a prearranged disbursement plan?
- made only after reviewing written inspection reports?

- subject to advance, written authorization by the
  - contractor?
  - borrower?
  - inspector?
  - lending officer?
- reviewed by a bank employee who had no part in granting the loan?
- compared with original cost estimates?
- checked against previous disbursements?
- made directly to subcontractors?
- supported by receipted bills describing the work performed and the materials furnished?

85. Does the bank update its title policy by obtaining a "date down" endorsement with each draw?

86. Does the bank obtain waivers of subcontractors' and materialmen's liens as work is completed and disbursements made?

87. Are periodic reviews made of undisbursed loan proceeds to determine their adequacy to complete the projects?

88. Does the bank confirm that a certificate of occupancy has been obtained before final disbursement?

89. Does the bank obtain sworn and notarized releases of mechanics' liens at the time construction is completed and before final disbursement?

90. Are independent proofs made at least monthly of undisbursed loan proceeds and contingency or escrow accounts? Are statements on such accounts regularly mailed to customers?

Take-Out Commitments

91. In the event loan repayment is dependent on take-out financing,

- are take-out agreements reviewed for acceptability by counsel?
- are financial statements obtained and reviewed to determine the financial responsibility of permanent lenders?
- is a tri-party buy and sell agreement signed before the construction loan is closed?
- does the bank require take-out agreements to include an "act of God" clause, which provides for an automatic extension of the completion date in the event that construction delays occur for reasons beyond the builder's control?
- does the bank accept stand-by commitments for "gap financing" of limited take-out commitments?

Completion Bonding Requirements

92. Does the bank require a completion insurance bond for all construction loans?

93. Does counsel review completion insurance bonds for acceptability?

94. Has the bank established minimum financial standards for borrowers who are not required to obtain completion bonding? Are the standards observed in all cases?

Documentation

95. Does the bank require and maintain documentary evidence of

- the contractor's payment of
  - employee withholding taxes?
  - builder's risk insurance?
  - workmen's compensation insurance?
  - public liability insurance?
- the property owner's payment of
  - real estate taxes?
  - hazard insurance premiums?

96. Does the bank require that documentation files include

- loan applications, if used?
- loan commitments?
- financial statements for the
  - borrower?
  - builder?
  - proposed prime tenant?
  - take-out lender?
  - guarantors?
- credit and trade checks on the
  - borrower?
  - builder?
  - major sub-contractor?
  - proposed tenants?
- a copy of plans and specifications?
- a copy of the building permit?
- a survey of the property?
- soil report?
- environmental assessment?
- loan commitment?
- loan agreement?

- appraisal or evaluation?
- mortgage or deed of trust?
- ground leases?
- assignment of tenant leases or letters of intent to lease?
- tenant estoppels?
- copies of any other legally binding agreements between the borrower and tenants?
- reports of past due leases, including delinquent expense reimbursements?
- a copy of take-out commitment, if applicable?
- a copy of the borrower's application to the take-out lender?
- a tri-party buy and sell agreement?
- inspection reports?
- disbursement authorizations?
- undisbursed loan proceeds and contingency or escrow account reconcilements?
- title and hazard insurance policies?
- evidence of zoning or a zoning endorsement to the title policy?
- evidence of the availability of utilities to the site?

97. Does the bank employ standardized checklists to control documentation for individual files?

98. Do documentation files note all of the borrower's other loan and deposit account relationships?

99. Does the bank use tickler files that

- control stage advance inspections and disbursements?
- assure prompt administrative follow-up on items sent for
  - recording?
  - attorney's opinion?
  - expert review?

100. Does the bank maintain tickler files that will provide at least 30 days advance notice before expiration of

- take-out commitment?
- hazard insurance?
- workmen's compensation insurance?
- public liability insurance?

Real Estate Loan Records

101. Is the preparation and posting of subsidiary real estate loan records performed or adequately supervised by persons who do not also

    - issue official checks or drafts singly?
    - handle cash?

102. Are the subsidiary real estate loan records reconciled daily with the appropriate general ledger accounts and are reconciling items investigated by persons who do not also handle cash?

103. Are loan statements, delinquent account collection requests, and past-due notices checked to the trial balances used in reconciling real estate loan subsidiary records to general ledger amounts, and are they handled only by persons who do not also handle cash?

104. Are inquiries about loan balances received and investigated by persons who do not also handle cash?

105. Are documents supporting recorded credit adjustments checked or tested subsequently by persons who do not also handle cash (if so, explain briefly)?

106. Is a daily record maintained summarizing note transaction details, that is, loans made, payments received, and interest collected, to support applicable general ledger account entries?

107. Are frequent note and liability ledger trial balances prepared and reconciled to controlling accounts by employees who do not process or record loan transactions?

108. Are subsidiary payment records and files pertaining to serviced loans segregated and identifiable?

109. Are properties under foreclosure proceedings segregated?

110. Is an overdue accounts report generated frequently? If so, how frequently?

Loan Interest and Commitment Fees

111. Is the preparation, addition, and posting of interest and fees records performed or reviewed by persons who do not also

    - issue official checks or drafts singly?
    - handle cash?

112. Are any independent interest and fee computations made and compared, or adequately tested, with initial interest records by persons who do not also

- issue official checks or drafts singly?
- handle cash?

113. Are fees and other charges collected in connection with real estate loans accounted for in accordance with ASC Subtopic 310-20, "Nonrefundable Fees and Other Costs"?

Other Areas of Interest

114. Does the bank take steps to determine whether there are any environmental hazards associated with the real estate proposed to be mortgaged? Are policies in place to ensure that the bank

- identifies, evaluates and monitors potential environmental risks associated with its lending operations?
- establishes procedures to determine the extent of due diligence necessary to protect the bank's business interests?
- assesses the potential adverse effect of environmental contamination on the value of real property securing its loans, including any potential environmental liability associated with foreclosing on contaminated properties?

115. When there is reason to believe that there may be serious environmental problems associated with property that it holds as collateral, does the bank

- take steps to monitor the situation so as to minimize any potential liability on the part of the bank?
- seek the advice of experts, particularly in situations where the bank may be considering foreclosure on the contaminated property?

116. Are all real estate loan commitments issued in written form?

117. Are loan officers prohibited from processing loan payments?

118. Is the receipt of loan payments by mail recorded upon receipt independently before being sent to and processed by a note teller?

119. Regarding mortgage documents,

- has the responsibility for the document files been established?
- does the bank utilize a check sheet to assure that required documents are received and on file?
- are safeguards in effect to protect notes and other documents?
- does the bank obtain a signed application form for all real estate mortgage loan requests?
- are separate credit files maintained?

- is there a program of systematic follow-up to determine that all required documents are received?
- does a designated employee conduct a review after loan closing to determine if all documents are properly drawn, executed, and in the bank's files?
- are all notes and other instruments pertaining to paid-off loans returned promptly to the borrower, cancelled and marked paid, where appropriate?

120. Regarding insurance coverage,

- does the bank have a mortgage errors and omissions policy?
- is there a procedure for determining that insurance premiums are current on properties securing loans?
- does the bank require that the policies include a loss payable clause to the bank?
- are escrow accounts reviewed at least annually to determine if monthly deposits cover anticipated disbursements?
- do records showing the nature and purpose of the disbursement support disbursements for taxes and insurance?
- if advance deposits for taxes and insurance are not required, does the bank have a system to determine that taxes and insurance are being paid?

121. Are properties to which the bank has obtained title immediately transferred to the "other real estate owned" account?

122. Does the bank have a written schedule of fees, rates, terms, and types of collateral for all new loans?

123. Are approvals of real estate advances reviewed, before disbursement, to determine that such advances do not increase the borrower's total liability to an amount in excess of the bank's legal lending limit?

124. Are procedures in effect to ensure compliance with the requirements of government agencies insuring or guaranteeing loans?

125. Are detailed statements of account balances and activity mailed to mortgagors at least annually?

Conclusion

126. Is the foregoing information an adequate basis for evaluating internal controls? Are there any significant additional internal auditing procedures, accounting controls, administrative controls, or other circumstances that impair any controls or mitigate any weaknesses indicated above (explain negative answers briefly, and indicate conclusions as to their effect on specific examination or verification procedures)?[18]

127. Based on the answers to the foregoing questions, internal control for CRE lending is considered (strong, satisfactory, weak).

---

[18] See the "Loan Portfolio Management" booklet of the *Comptroller's Handbook* regarding the evaluation of the adequacy of loan review and loan-related audit reports.

Verification Procedures

Verification procedures are used to verify the existence of assets and liabilities, or test the reliability of financial records. Examiners generally do not perform verification procedures as part of a typical examination. Rather, verification procedures are performed when substantive safety and soundness concerns are identified that are not mitigated by the bank's risk management systems and internal controls.

1. Reconcile the trial balance to the general ledger. Include loan commitments and other contingent liabilities in the testing.

2. Using an appropriate sampling technique, select loans from the trial balance and

   - prepare and mail confirmation forms to borrowers. (Loans serviced by other institutions, either whole loans or participations, should be confirmed only with the servicing institution. Loans serviced for other institutions, either whole loans or participations, should be confirmed with the other institution and the borrower. Confirmation forms should include the borrower's name, loan number, original amount, interest rate, current loan balance, contingency and escrow account balance, and a brief description of the collateral.)
     - After a reasonable time period, mail second requests.
     - Follow up on any no-replies or exceptions and resolve differences.

   - examine notes for completeness and reconcile date, amount, and terms to trial balance.
     - In the event any notes are not held at the bank, request confirmation with the holder.
     - See that required initials of approving officer are on the note.
     - See that the note is signed, appears to be genuine, and is negotiable.

   - compare collateral held in files with the description on the collateral register. List and investigate all collateral discrepancies.

   - determine if any collateral is held by an outside custodian or has been temporarily removed for any reason. Request confirmation for any collateral held outside the bank.

   - determine that each file contains documentation supporting guarantees and subordination agreements, where appropriate.

   - determine that any required insurance coverage is adequate and that the bank is named as loss payee.

- review participation agreements making excerpts, when deemed necessary, for such items as rate of service fee, interest rate, retention of late charges, and remittance requirements, and determine whether the customer has complied.

- review loan agreement provisions for hold back or retention, and determine if undisbursed loan funds or contingency or escrow accounts are equal to retention or hold-back requirements.

- if separate reserves are maintained, determine if debit entries to those accounts are authorized in accordance with the terms of the loan agreement and if they are supported by inspection reports, certificates of completion, individual bills, or other evidence.

- review disbursement ledgers and authorizations, and determine if authorizations are signed in accordance with the terms of the loan agreement.

- reconcile debits in the undisbursed loan proceeds accounts to inspection reports, individual bills, or other evidence supporting disbursements.

3. Review the accrued interest accounts, and

    - review procedures for accounting for accrued interest and handling of adjustments.
    - scan accrued interest and income accounts for any unusual entries and follow up on any unusual items by tracing to initial and supporting records.

4. Obtain or prepare a schedule showing the amount of monthly interest income and the real estate loan balances at the end of each month since the last examination, and

    - calculate or check yield.
    - investigate significant fluctuations or trends.

5. Using a list of nonaccruing loans, check loan accrual records to determine that interest income is not being accrued.

Appendixes

Appendix A: Quantity of Credit Risk Indicators

Examiners should consider the following indicators when assessing the effect of CRE lending activities on credit risk.

Low	Moderate	High
The level of CRE loans outstanding is low relative to capital.	The level of CRE loans outstanding is moderate relative to capital.	The level of CRE loans outstanding is high relative to capital.
CRE growth rates are supported by local, regional, or national economic trends. Growth, including off-balance-sheet activities, has been planned for and is commensurate with management and staff expertise, as well as operational capabilities.	CRE growth rates exceed local, regional, or national economic trends. Growth, including off-balance-sheet activities, has not been planned for or exceeds planned levels and may test the capabilities of management, credit staff, and MIS.	CRE growth rates significantly exceed local, regional, or national economic trends. Growth, including off-balance-sheet activities, has not been planned for or exceeds planned levels and stretches the experience and capability of management, credit staff, and MIS. Growth may also be in new products or outside the bank's traditional lending area.
Interest and fee income from CRE lending activities is not a significant portion of loan income.	Interest and fee income from CRE lending activities is an important component of loan income; however, the bank's lending activities remain diversified.	The bank is highly dependent upon interest and fees from CRE lending activities. Management may seek higher returns through higher risk product or customer types. Loan yields may be disproportionate relative to risk.
The bank's CRE portfolio is well diversified with no single large concentrations or a few moderate concentrations. Concentrations are well within reasonable internal limits. The CRE portfolio mix does not materially affect the risk profile.	The bank has a few material CRE concentrations that may be approaching internal limits. The CRE portfolio mix may increase the bank's credit-risk profile.	The bank has large CRE concentrations that may exceed internal limits. The CRE portfolio mix increases the bank's credit-risk profile.
CRE underwriting is conservative. Policies and procedures are reasonable. CRE loans with structural weaknesses or underwriting exceptions are occasionally originated; however, the weaknesses are effectively mitigated.	CRE underwriting is satisfactory. The bank has an average level of CRE loans with structural weaknesses or exceptions to underwriting standards. Exceptions are reasonably mitigated and consistent with competitive pressures and reasonable growth objectives.	CRE underwriting is liberal and policies are inadequate. The bank has a high level of CRE loans with structural weaknesses or underwriting exceptions the volume of which expose the bank to loss in the event of default.

Low	Moderate	High
Collateral requirements for CRE loans are conservative. Appraisals and evaluations are reasonable, timely, and well supported. Reviews are appropriate and reliable.	Collateral requirements for CRE loans are acceptable. Some collateral exceptions exist, but are reasonably mitigated and monitored. A moderate volume of appraisals or evaluations are not well supported or are not always obtained in a timely manner. A moderate volume of reviews may not be appropriate or reliable.	Collateral requirements for CRE loans are liberal, or if policies are conservative, substantial deviations exist. Appraisals and evaluations are not always obtained, frequently unsupported or unreliable, or reflect inadequate protection. Updated appraisals or evaluations are not obtained in a timely manner. Reviews are often not performed or are inadequate.
CRE loan documentation or collateral exceptions are low and have minimal effect on the bank's risk profile.	The level of CRE loan documentation or collateral exceptions is moderate; however, exceptions are reasonably mitigated and corrected in a timely manner, if applicable. The risk of loss from these exceptions is not material.	The level of CRE loan documentation or collateral exceptions is high. Exceptions are not mitigated and not corrected in a timely manner. The risk of loss from the exceptions is heightened.
CRE loan distribution across the pass category is consistent with a conservative risk appetite. Migration trends within the pass category favor the less risky ratings. Lagging indicators, including past dues and nonaccruals, are low and stable.	CRE loan distribution across the pass category is consistent with a moderate risk appetite. Migration trends within the pass category may favor riskier ratings. Lagging indicators, including past dues and nonaccruals, are moderate and may be slightly increasing.	CRE loan distribution across the pass category is heavily skewed toward riskier pass ratings. Lagging indicators, including past dues and nonaccruals, are moderate or high and the trend is increasing.
The volume of classified and special mention CRE loans is low and is not skewed toward more severe risk ratings.	The volume of classified and Special Mention CRE loans is moderate, but is not skewed toward more severe ratings.	The volume of classified and special mention CRE loans is moderate or high, skewed to the more severe ratings, and increasing.
CRE refinancing and renewal practices raise little or no concern regarding the quality of CRE loans and the accuracy of reported problem loan data.	CRE refinancing and renewal practices pose some concern regarding the quality of CRE loans and the accuracy of reported problem loan data.	CRE refinancing and renewal practices raise substantial concerns regarding the quality of CRE loans and the accuracy of reported problem loan data.
The volume of CRE loans with environmental concerns is not significant. Environmental evaluations are timely, appropriate, and well supported.	The volume of CRE loans with environmental concerns is moderate; however, the risks are identified and reasonably mitigated. Environmental evaluations are not always performed in a timely manner.	The volume of CRE loans with environmental concerns is material if left uncorrected. Environmental evaluations are not performed in a timely manner, or management's response to identified environmental concerns is not appropriate.

Appendix B: Quality of Credit Risk Management Indicators

Examiners should consider the following indicators when assessing the effect of CRE lending activities on credit risk management.

Strong	Satisfactory	Weak
There is a clear, sound CRE credit culture. Board and management tolerance for risk is well communicated and fully understood.	The intent of CRE lending activities is generally understood, but the culture and risk tolerances may not be clearly communicated or uniformly implemented throughout the institution.	The CRE credit culture is absent or is materially flawed. Risk tolerances may not be well understood.
CRE initiatives are consistent with a conservative risk appetite and promote an appropriate balance between risk-taking and strategic objectives. New CRE loan products are well researched, tested, and approved before implementation.	CRE initiatives are consistent with a moderate risk appetite. Generally, there is an appropriate balance between risk-taking and strategic objectives; however, anxiety for income may lead to higher-risk transactions. New CRE loan products may be implemented without sufficient testing, but risks are generally understood.	CRE initiatives are liberal and encourage risk-taking. Anxiety for income dominates planning activities. New CRE loan products are implemented without conducting sufficient due diligence.
The appraisal and evaluation program is fully effective. Policies and procedures faithfully reflect relevant guidance and controls are sufficient to ensure their consistent implementation. Staff responsible for performing or oversight of appraisals, evaluations, and reviews are competent, independent, and have the appropriate experience and training.	The appraisal and evaluation program is effective in most respects but improvement is needed in one or more areas such as ensuring sufficient personnel, independence, review, engagement, or collateral monitoring; policies and procedures may require some modification or some improvement may be needed. Staff may require additional training in some areas.	The appraisal and evaluation program is ineffective. Policies and procedures do not adequately reflect regulations or guidance or are not implemented. Staff performing appraisal-related duties does not have sufficient training or experience. Collateral values in general may be unreliable.
Management is effective. The CRE lending staff possesses sufficient expertise to effectively administer the risk assumed. Responsibilities and accountability are clear, and appropriate remedial or corrective action is taken when needed.	Management satisfactorily manages CRE risk, but improvement may be needed in one or more areas. CRE staff generally possesses the expertise to administer assumed risks; however, additional expertise may be required in one or more areas. Responsibilities and accountability may require some clarification. In general, appropriate remedial or corrective action is taken when needed.	CRE risk management is deficient. CRE staff may not possess sufficient expertise, or may demonstrate an unwillingness to effectively administer the risk assumed. Responsibilities and accountability may not be clear. Corrective actions are insufficient to address root causes of problems.

Strong	**Satisfactory**	**Weak**
Diversification management is effective. CRE concentration limits are set at reasonable levels. CRE concentration risk-management practices are sound, including management's efforts to reduce or mitigate exposures. Management effectively identifies and understands correlated risk exposures and their potential effect.	Diversification management is adequate, but certain aspects may need improvement. CRE concentrations are identified and reported, but limits and other action triggers may be absent or moderately high. Concentration management efforts may be focused at the individual loan level, while portfolio level efforts may be inadequate. Correlated exposures may not be identified and their risks not fully understood.	Diversification management is passive or deficient. Management may not identify concentrations, or take little or no action to reduce, limit, or mitigate the associated risk. Limits may be established but represent a significant portion of capital. Management may not understand exposure correlations and their potential effect. Concentration limits may be exceeded or raised frequently.
Loan management and personnel compensation structures provide appropriate balance between loan or revenue production, loan quality, and portfolio administration, including risk identification.	Loan management and personnel compensation structures provide reasonable balance between loan or revenue production, loan quality, and portfolio administration.	Loan management and personnel compensation structures are skewed to loan or revenue production. There is little evidence of substantive incentives or accountability for loan quality and portfolio administration.
CRE staffing levels and expertise are appropriate for the size and complexity of CRE activities. Staff turnover is low and the transfer of responsibilities is orderly. Training programs facilitate ongoing staff development.	CRE staffing levels and expertise are generally adequate for the size and complexity of CRE activities. Staff turnover is moderate and may result in some temporary gaps in portfolio management. Training initiatives are adequate.	CRE staffing levels and expertise are deficient. Turnover is high. Management does not provide sufficient resources for staff training.
CRE lending policies effectively establish and communicate portfolio objectives, risk tolerances, loan underwriting standards and risk-selection standards.	CRE lending policies are fundamentally adequate. Enhancement, while generally not critical, can be achieved in one or more areas. Specificity of risk tolerance or underwriting standards may need improvement to fully communicate policy requirements.	CRE lending policies are deficient in one or more ways and require significant improvements. Policies may not be clear or are too general to adequately communicate portfolio objectives, risk tolerances, and underwriting and risk selection standards.
Staff effectively identifies, approves, tracks, and reports significant policy, underwriting, and risk-selection exceptions individually and in aggregate, including risk exposures associated with off-balance-sheet activities.	Staff identifies, approves, and reports significant policy, underwriting, and risk-selection exceptions on a loan-by-loan basis, including risk exposures associated with off-balance-sheet activities. Little aggregation or trend analysis is conducted, however, to determine the effect on portfolio quality.	Policy exceptions may not receive appropriate approval, significant policy exceptions may be approved but not reported individually or in aggregate, or their effect on portfolio quality is not analyzed. Risk exposures associated with off-balance-sheet activities may not be considered.
Credit analysis is thorough and timely both at underwriting and periodically thereafter.	Credit analysis appropriately identifies key risks and is conducted within reasonable time frames. Post-underwriting analysis may need some strengthening.	Credit analysis is deficient. Analysis is superficial and key risks are overlooked. Credit data are not reviewed in a timely manner.

Strong	**Satisfactory**	**Weak**
Risk rating and problem loan review and identification systems are accurate and timely. Credit risk is effectively stratified for both problem and pass credits. Systems serve as effective early warning tools and support risk-based pricing, the ALLL, and capital allocations.	Risk rating and problem loan review and identification systems are adequate. Problem and emerging problem credits are adequately identified, although room for improvement exists. The number of rating categories for pass credits may need to be expanded to facilitate early warning, risk-based pricing, or capital allocations.	Risk rating and problem loan review and identification systems are deficient. Problem credits may not be identified accurately or in a timely manner resulting in misstated levels of portfolio risk. The number of rating categories for pass credits is insufficient to stratify risk for early warning or other purposes.
Special mention ratings do not indicate any administration issues within the CRE portfolio.	Special mention ratings generally do not indicate administration issues within the CRE portfolio.	Special mention ratings indicate management is not properly administering the CRE portfolio.
MIS provides accurate, timely, and complete CRE portfolio information. Management and the board receive appropriate reports to analyze and understand the effect of CRE activities on the bank's credit risk profile, including off-balance-sheet activities. MIS facilitate timely exception reporting.	MIS is adequate. Management and the board generally receive appropriate reports to analyze and understand the effect of CRE activities on the bank's credit-risk profile; however, modest improvement may be needed in one or more areas. MIS facilitate generally timely exception reporting.	MIS is deficient. The accuracy or timeliness of information may be affected in a material way. Management and the board may not be receiving sufficient information to analyze and understand the effect of CRE activities on the bank's credit-risk profile. Exception reporting requires improvement.

Appendix C: Glossary

Entries marked with an asterisk (*) are as defined in the "Interagency Guidelines for Real Estate Lending Policies." Entries marked with a double asterisk (**) are as defined in the "Interagency Appraisal and Evaluation Guidelines."

Appraisal:** A written statement independently and impartially prepared by a qualified appraiser (state licensed or certified) setting forth an opinion as to the market value of an adequately described property as of a specific date(s), supported by the presentation and analysis of relevant market information.

"As-complete" market value: See prospective market value.

"As-is" market value:** The estimate of the market value of real property in its current physical condition, use, and zoning as of the appraisal's effective date.

"As-stabilized" market value: See prospective market value.

Broker price opinion (BPO):** An estimate of the probable sales or listing price of the subject property provided by a real estate broker, sales agent, or sales person. A BPO generally provides a varying level of detail about a property's condition, market, and neighborhood, as well as comparable sales or listings. A BPO is not by itself an appraisal or evaluation, but could be used for monitoring the collateral value of an existing loan, when deemed appropriate.

Capitalization rate: Rate used to convert income into value. Specifically, it is the ratio between a property's stabilized NOI and the property's sales price. Sometimes referred to as an overall rate because it can be computed as a weighted average of component investment claims on NOI.

Construction loan:* An extension of credit for the purpose of erecting or rehabilitating buildings or other structures, including any infrastructure necessary for development.

Debt-service coverage ratio: Cash flow or NOI divided by the debt service.

Discount rate: A rate of return used to convert future payments or receipts into their present value.

Effective gross income: The expected revenue generated by a property after the application of a vacancy rate and deductions for expected credit losses. See also "Gross Income."

Evaluation:** A valuation permitted by the appraisal regulations for transactions that qualify for the appraisal threshold exemption, business loan exemption, or subsequent transaction exemption.

Exposure time: The estimated length of time the property interest being appraised would have been offered on the market before the hypothetical consummation of a sale at market value on the effective date of the appraisal. Exposure time is always presumed to precede the effective date of the appraisal. Exposure time is a function of price, time, and use—not an isolated opinion of time alone.[19]

Extension of credit or loan:*

- The total amount of any loan, line of credit, or other legally binding lending commitment with respect to real property; and
- The total amount, based on the amount of consideration paid, of any loan, line of credit, or other legally binding lending commitment acquired by a lender by purchase, assignment, or otherwise.

Federally related transaction:* Any real estate-related financial transaction in which any regulated institution engages or contracts for, and that requires the services of an appraiser. See also "Real Estate-Related Financial Transaction."

Going concern value:* The value of a business entity rather than the value of the real property. The valuation is based on the existing operations of the business and its current operating record, with the assumption that the business will continue to operate.

Gross lease: A lease agreement wherein the landlord is responsible for the payment of property operating expenses. Because even gross leases often require some expenses to be paid by the tenant, the lease itself should always be analyzed. This analysis is critical to developing an accurate estimate of cash flow and NOI for the property.

Gross income: The revenue generated by a property assuming full occupancy and before the application of a vacancy rate and deductions for expected credit losses. See also "Effective Gross Income."

Hard equity: A borrower's tangible equity invested in a property including cash, unencumbered real estate (e.g., land) and materials for improvements.

Improved property loan:* An extension of credit secured by one of the following types of real property:

- Farmland, ranchland, or timberland committed to ongoing management and agricultural production.
- One- to four-family residential property that is not owner-occupied.
- Residential property containing five or more individual dwelling units.
- Completed commercial property.

---

[19] *Uniform Standards of Professional Appraisal Practice*, Appraisal Standards Board, The Appraisal Foundation, 2012-2013 Edition.

- Other income-producing property that has been completed and is available for occupancy and use, except income-producing owner-occupied one- to four-family residential property.

Land development loan:* An extension of credit for the purpose of improving unimproved real property before the erection of structures. The improvement of unimproved real property may include the laying or placement of sewers, water pipes, utility cables, streets, and other infrastructure necessary for future development. (Loans secured by already improved residential building lots are subject to the same 75 percent LTV as land development loans.)

Loan origination date:* The time of inception of the obligation to extend credit (i.e., when the last event or prerequisite, controllable by the lender, occurs, causing the lender to become legally bound to fund an extension of credit).

Loan-to-value or **loan-to-value ratio:*** The percentage or ratio that is derived at the time of loan origination by dividing an extension of credit by the total market value of the property(ies) securing or being improved by the extension of credit, plus the amount of any readily marketable or other acceptable non-real estate collateral. The total amount of all senior liens on or interests in such property(ies) should be included in determining the LTV ratio. When mortgage insurance or collateral is used in the calculation of the LTV ratio, and such credit enhancement is later released or replaced, the LTV ratio should be recalculated.

Market value:** The most probable price which a property should bring in a competitive and open market under all conditions requisite to a fair sale, the buyer and seller each acting prudently and knowledgeably, and assuming the price is not affected by undue stimulus. Implicit in this definition are the consummation of a sale as of a specified date and the passing of title from seller to buyer under conditions whereby

- buyer and seller are typically motivated.
- both parties are well informed or well advised and acting in what they consider their own best interests.
- a reasonable time is allowed for exposure in the open market.
- payment is made in terms of cash in U.S. dollars or in terms of financial arrangements comparable thereto.
- the price represents the normal consideration for the property sold unaffected by special or creative financing or sales concessions granted by anyone associated with the sale.

Marketing period or **marketing time:** The time it might take to sell the property interest at the appraised market value during the period immediately after the effective date of the appraisal.

Mezzanine loan: In CRE, a loan that is secured by an assignment of an equity interest rather than a collateral interest in the property.

Net lease: A lease agreement wherein the tenant must pay operating expenses, either directly or by reimbursement to the landlord. Net leases may be referred to as net, double net (NN), triple net (NNN), or absolute net. Because these terms lack universally agreed upon definitions, the lease itself should always be analyzed to determine the expenses for which a landlord or tenant is responsible rather than relying on these terms. This determination is critical to developing an accurate estimate of cash flow and NOI for the property.

Net operating income (NOI): Annual gross income less operating expenses. Gross income includes all income generated through the operation of the property. In addition to rents, it may include other income such as parking fees and laundry and vending. Tenant reimbursements may also be included if the reimbursed expenses are included in the operating expenses. Operating expenses are the costs incurred in the operation and normal maintenance of a property. They do not include interest, principal, or income taxes. While operating expenses do not include depreciation or capital items, they do include a reserve for the replacement of capital items (replacement reserve). The replacement reserve is imputed for underwriting purposes irrespective of whether it is actually funded.

To determine a property's stabilized NOI for underwriting purposes, the analysis begins with determining the gross income that a property would generate when fully leased. This is then adjusted by the application of a vacancy factor to arrive at the Effective Gross Income. The vacancy factor may be higher or lower than actual and represents an estimate of the vacancy that the property is expected to experience throughout the life of the property. The selection of a vacancy factor should consider vacancies in comparable properties in the same market. Variable operating expenses that are directly related to occupancy may also be adjusted to reflect the vacancy assumptions

One- to four-family residential property:* Property containing fewer than five individual dwelling units, including manufactured homes permanently affixed to the underlying property (when deemed to be real property under state law).

Owner-occupied: A property is owner-occupied when the primary source of repayment is not derived from third party, nonaffiliated, rental income associated with the property (i.e., any such rental income is less than 50 percent of the source of repayment).

Presold unit:** A unit may be considered presold if a buyer has entered into a binding contract to purchase the unit and has made a substantial and nonrefundable earnest money deposit. Further, the institution should obtain sufficient documentation that the buyer has entered into a legally binding sales contract and has obtained a written prequalification or commitment for permanent financing.

Prospective market value "as-completed" and "as-stabilized":** According to the USPAP, an appraisal with a prospective market value reflects an effective date that is subsequent to the date of the appraisal report. A prospective market value may be appropriate for the valuation of a property interest related to a credit decision for a proposed development or renovation project. Prospective value opinions are intended to reflect the current expectations and perceptions of market participants, based on available data. Two prospective value opinions may be required to reflect the time frame during which development, construction, and occupancy occur. The prospective market value "as-completed" reflects the property's market value as of the time that development is expected to be completed. The prospective market value "as stabilized" reflects the property's market value as of the time the property is projected to achieve stabilized occupancy. For an income-producing property, stabilized occupancy is the occupancy level that a property is expected to achieve after the property is exposed to the market for lease over a reasonable period of time and at comparable terms and conditions to other similar properties.

Readily marketable collateral:* Insured deposits, financial instruments, and bullion in which the lender has a perfected interest. Financial instruments and bullion must be salable under ordinary circumstances with reasonable promptness at a fair market value determined by quotations based on actual transactions, on an auction or similarly available daily bid and ask price market. Readily marketable collateral should be appropriately discounted by the lender consistent with the lender's usual practices for making loans secured by such collateral. Examples of readily marketable financial instruments include stocks, bonds, debentures, commercial paper, negotiable certificates of deposit, and shares in mutual funds.

Real estate-related financial transaction:** Any transaction involving the sale, lease, purchase, investment in or exchange of real property, including interests in property, or the financing thereof; the refinancing of real property or interests in real property; or the use of real property or interests in property as security for a loan or investment, including mortgage-backed securities.

Replacement reserves: A reserve for the periodic replacement of such capital items as heating, ventilation, and air conditioning (HVAC), roof, and parking lots. A lender may or may not require that these reserves be funded. Although not a cash expense in all periods, however, reserves for replacement should be deducted from income in determining NOI.

Reversion value or **terminal value:** The lump-sum amount an investor expects to receive when an investment is sold. In real estate appraisal, the reversion, or terminal value, is determined by capitalizing the projected NOI for the last year of the holding period. This value is then discounted back to present value at the chosen discount rate and added to the net present value of the periodic cash flows.

Value:* An opinion or estimate, set forth in an appraisal or evaluation, whichever may be appropriate, of the market value of real property, prepared in accordance with appraisal regulations and guidance. For loans to purchase an existing property, the term "value" means the lesser of the actual acquisition cost or the estimate of value.

References

Laws

12 USC 371, "Real Estate Loans" (national banks)
12 USC 1464(c), "Federal Savings Associations, Loans and Investments"

Regulations

Appraisals
12 CFR 34, subpart C, "Appraisals" (national banks) and 12 CFR 164,"Appraisals" (federal savings associations)

Authority
12 CFR 7.1006, subpart A, "Bank Powers—Loan agreement providing for a share in profits, income, or earnings or for stock warrants" (national banks)

12 CFR 160.30, "General Lending and Investment Powers of Federal Savings Associations" (federal savings associations)

12 CFR 159.5, "Subordinate Organizations—How much may a federal savings association invest in service corporations or lower-tier entities?" (federal savings associations)

Capital
12 CFR 3.2(e), "Definitions—Total Capital" (national banks) and 12 CFR 167.5, "Components of Capital—Total Capital" (federal savings associations)

Safety and Soundness Standards
12 CFR 30 (national banks) and 12 CFR 170, appendix A (federal savings associations), "Interagency Guidelines for Establishing Standards for Safety and Soundness"

Real Estate Lending Standards
12 CFR 34, subpart D (national banks) and 12 CFR 160.101(federal savings associations), "Real Estate Lending Standards"

Interagency Guidelines for Real Estate Lending Policies
12 CFR 34, subpart D, appendix A "Interagency Guidelines for Real Estate Lending" (national banks) and appendix to12 CFR 160.101, "Interagency Guidelines for Real Estate Lending Policies" (federal savings associations)

Comptroller's Handbook

Examination Process
"Bank Supervision Process"
"Community Bank Supervision"
"Federal Branches and Agencies Supervision"
"Large Bank Supervision"
"Sampling Methodologies"

Safety and Soundness, Asset Quality
"Allowance for Loan and Lease Losses"
"Concentrations of Credit"
"Loan Portfolio Management"
"Other Real Estate Owned"
"Rating Credit Risk"

Safety and Soundness, Liquidity
"Liquidity"

OCC Issuances

Bank Accounting Advisory Series
OCC Bulletin 2012-33, "Community Bank Stress Testing: Supervisory Guidance" (October 18, 2012)
OCC Bulletin 2012-16, "Capital Planning: Guidance for Evaluating Capital Planning and Adequacy" (June 7, 2012)
OCC Bulletin 2012-14, "Stress Testing: Interagency Stress Testing Guidance" (May 14, 2012)
OCC Bulletin 2012-10, "Troubled Debt Restructurings: Supervisory Guidance on Accounting and Reporting Requirements" (April 5, 2012)
OCC Bulletin 2010-42, "Sound Practices for Appraisals and Evaluations: Interagency Appraisal and Evaluation Guidelines" (December 10, 2010)
OCC Bulletin 2010-24: "Incentive Compensation: Interagency Guidance on Sound Incentive Compensation Policies" (June 30, 2010)
OCC Bulletin 2009-32, "Commercial Real Estate (CRE) Loans: Guidance on Prudent CRE Loan Workouts" (October 30, 2009)
OCC Bulletin 2006-47, "Allowance for Loan and Lease Losses (ALLL): Guidance and Frequently Asked Questions (FAQs) on the ALLL" (December 13, 2006)
OCC Bulletin 2006-46, "Concentrations in Commercial Real Estate Lending, Sound Risk Management Practices: Interagency Guidance on CRE Concentration Risk Management" (December 6, 2006)
OCC Bulletin 2005- 32, "Frequently Asked Questions: Residential Tract Development Lending" (September 8, 2005)
OCC Bulletin 2005-6, "Appraisal Regulations and the Interagency Statement on Independent Appraisal and Evaluation Functions: Frequently Asked Questions" (March 22, 2005)

OCC Bulletin 2001-37, "Policy Statement on Allowance for Loan and Lease Losses Methodologies and Documentation for Banks and Savings Institutions: ALLL Methodologies and Documentation" (July 20, 2001)

Thrift Bulletin 78a, "Investment Limitations under the Home Owners' Loan Act" (December 8, 2003)

Other

Accounting Standards Codification

ASC Topic 310, "Receivables"

ASC Topic 970, "Real Estate—General"

ASC Topic 974, "Real Estate—Real Estate Investment Trusts"

ASC Subtopic 450-20, "Loss Contingencies"

Uniform Standards of Professional Appraisal Practice (USPAP)

www.ingramcontent.com/pod-product-compliance
Lightning Source LLC
Chambersburg PA
CBHW080257290526
45790CB00005B/1843